JEANIE O'HARE

Jeanie O'Hare is Director of New Work Development at The
Public Theater in New York. She was Chair of Playwriting at
the Yale School of Drama from 2012–16, and Company
Dramaturg for the Royal Shakespeare Company for seven
years. During that time she worked on classics, new plays and
musicals, including the commissioning and development of
Matilda the Musical. She was Literary Manager of Hampstead
Theatre from 2001–4. She trained at the Royal Court Theatre
under Artistic Director Stephen Daldry from 1994–2000. She
originally trained to be a sculptor.

Other Titles in this Series

Jeanie O'Hare

QUEEN MARGARET

taken from William Shakespeare

NICK HERN BOOKS

London

www.nickhernbooks.co.uk

A Nick Hern Book

Queen Margaret first published in Great Britain in 2018 as a paperback original by Nick Hern Books Limited, The Glasshouse, 49a Goldhawk Road, London W12 8QP

Queen Margaret copyright © 2018 Jeanie O'Hare

Jeanie O'Hare has asserted her moral rights to be identified as the author of this work

Cover photograph: Jade Anouka by Lee Baxter

Designed and typeset by Nick Hern Books, London
Printed in the UK by Mimeo Ltd, Huntingdon, Cambridgeshire PE29 6XX

A CIP catalogue record for this book is available from the British Library

ISBN   978 1 84842 810 2

Woodland
CARBON
www.woodlandcarbon.co.uk
NICK HERN BOOKS
Printed on Carbon Captured paper

Introduction
Jeanie O'Hare

I admit it took me a while to give myself permission to do this project. We English are very squeamish about altering Shakespeare. Our cousins in Germany thrive on radical undoings of our scared son, but we cross our arms and say no. I started thinking about making this play when I was working at the Royal Shakespeare Company ten years ago. Queen Margaret thumped me in the heart as I watched Katy Stephens' performance in Michael Boyd's production of the Complete History Cycle. She then nagged at me every day as I nodded to the enormous photo of Peggy Ashcroft in full battledress in the reception of the RSC's London offices. If I did what I wanted to do, some people would get upset – we know who they are – and there wasn't an anticipated slur that didn't curdle my blood at 4 a.m. for many a night.

But still the idea wouldn't go away. Permission came from knowing some of Shakespeare's history plays were already a collaboration. Marlowe is probably in there, and possibly other hands too. To join the collaboration was surely not a crime. Then the Manchester's Royal Exchange offered me a commission, and at last the opportunity to put this idea to the test had arrived.

For me, *Queen Margaret* is the history play that has been there in plain sight for four hundred years. Shakespeare wrote more lines for her than he did for King Lear, but because they are scattered across four plays (*Henry VI, Parts One, Two* and *Three*, and *Richard III*), the first three of which are very rarely performed, she remains largely unknown. She ruled England for over twenty years, but hardly a soul has heard of her. She is too important a role to be left unperformed, or, perhaps even worse, left in tatters yet again in another boys-own edit of the War of the Roses.

When I started I had a series of scenes, but not a play. My approach was in part that of a jeweller, creating a setting for the precious stones that were the set-piece scenes: the throne room, the killing of York, the death of the prince. To create this setting and allow the scenes to deliver their full emotional kick and consequence I had to create supporting material. I gave myself three rules: to use only words that were available to Shakespeare; only use images from his vast image bank; and only explore themes that he explored. Nothing contemporary would be imposed on the play.

So to write this additional material the question of verse inevitably came up. Surely I wasn't going to write in iambic pentameter? The answer is yes and no. The way I have written it is to trust the human body in the same way Shakespeare did. So an iamb is the beat of the human heart, 'de-dum de-dum', and the five double beats in a line are what you can comfortably say on one lungful of air. The pentameter is Shakespeare's heart at rest. When he gets excited, or sad, or aroused, he disrupts the rhythm of what he says, exactly as we do in everyday speech. We naturally talk in an underlying rough pentameter in the English language. We naturally break it when we shout or cry, or when our breathing and heartbeat are disrupted by love.

The other thing (which, if I am honest, it hurt to do) was take out all of the 'forsooths' and 'thees' and 'thous'. Often these are filler words, used when Shakespeare is slavishly trying to make up the right number of syllables for a line. If you strip the text of this layer of clutter, the modernity of what is left is striking. Then adding in new text is still daunting – but less impossible.

The War of the Roses is fundamentally a clash of families (*Game of Thrones*' Starks and Lannisters are based closely on the Yorks and the Lancasters), so I needed to find out the family background that Margaret was bringing to this fight. Her grandmother was Yolanda of Aragon, the patron of Joan of Arc and the mother-in-law of the French King. Yolanda had political reach across all of France and knew how to wield power. Margaret would have grown up witnessing political machinations, thinking about Joan morning, noon and night, and understanding how symbolism and divine right are central to monarchy. Yolanda also belonged to a tradition of women warriors of France, Eleanor of Aquitaine being chief amongst them – a warrior queen also married to an English king.

Although I have not imposed a contemporary sensibility onto the play, there is one deliberate twentieth-century addition. The Battle of Towton was the greatest loss of English lives in a single day until the first day of the Somme. The Towton hymn is based on a First World War poem by Canadian poet Marjorie Lowry Pickthall called 'Marching Men'. Pickthall, writing in 1922, was reaching back into medieval warfare to find an image for that slaughter. Adrienne Quartly, our composer and sound designer, has written the music for a hymn based on her words.

When we began rehearsing this two-hour play about the civil war in England, the Brexit parallels jumped out. The Cade Rebellion and Shakespeare's canny exploration of how elites use populism to gain power is starkly relevant to what we are currently living through. The play also taught me a lot about how European we really are. We have been a little bit French since that bloke from Normandy conquered us in 1066. Our kings had French as their mother tongue for generations. Writing in September 2018, with political chaos all around us, I am struck by the idea that we have decided our future whilst not really understanding our past.

With thanks to Jacob Robbins for story advice and the loan of his *Star Wars* figures, and to Elizabeth Freestone for everything.

Queen Margaret was first performed at the Royal Exchange Theatre, Manchester, on 14 September 2018, with the following cast:

QUEEN MARGARET	Jade Anouka
BAGOT / PRINCE EDWARD / RUTLAND	Islam Bouakkaz
YORK	Lorraine Bruce
SUFFOLK / CLIFFORD	Samuel Edward-Cook
EDWARD IV / CARDINAL	Dexter Flanders
HUME	Helena Lymbery
JOAN OF ARC	Lucy Mangan
SOMERSET / RICHARD	Kwami Odoom
GLOUCESTER / TUTOR	Roger Morlidge
WARWICK	Bridgitta Roy
HENRY VI	Max Runham
Director	Elizabeth Freestone
Designer	Amanda Stoodley
Lighting Designer	Johanna Town
Sound Designer/Composer	Adrienne Quartly
Movement Director	Vicki Manderson
Fight Director	Kenan Ali

For Sheila O'Hare
the original warrior queen

Characters

MARGARET *of Anjou, Queen to King Henry*
King HENRY *VI*
PRINCE EDWARD, *Prince of Wales, their son**

JOAN *of Arc*

Humphrey, Duke of GLOUCESTER, *uncle to Henry VI**
Earl of WARWICK, *first lord of the North, kingmaker*
CARDINAL *Beaufort, uncle to Henry VI*

Duke of YORK
EDWARD, *his son, later King Edward IV**
RICHARD, *also son to Duke of York, later Richard III**
Earl of RUTLAND, *son to Duke of York**

Duke of SOMERSET*
Duke of SUFFOLK*
Lord CLIFFORD*

HUME, *a petitioner, a page, a scribe, a pickpocket, a soldier,*
    a courtier
BAGOT, *a Petitioner**
TUTOR *to Rutland**

Chorus of attendants, messengers, soldiers, drummers, heralds

* *roles that must be doubled with a cast of eleven actors*

A forward slash (/) in the text marks the point at which the next
speaker interrupts, or continued speech.

This text went to press before the end of rehearsals and so may
differ slightly from the play as performed.

Prologue – Margaret Remembers France

London. The Parliament.

Enter MARGARET, *smoking a cigarette. Enter* JOAN.

JOAN.
King of England,
And you archers, foot soldiers, gentles and others,
Retire in God's name to your own country.
No man can take the throne of France by force.
Only God divines it so. Only God.

Sounds of battle.

The English have the field, the Frenchmen fly.
Now help me, familiar spirits
From the powerful regions about this earth,
Help me once more, that France may get the field.

Nothing.

O, hold me not with silence over-long!

Nothing.

My fallen soldiers cannot help me now.
This battlefield is scattered with their limbs.
Open heaven! That their souls may fly to God.

Nothing.

And here I stand alone, forsaken while
France must let her head fall into England's lap.
My holy incantations are too weak,
And hell is here,

Enter YORK.

with savage consequence.

YORK *attacks* JOAN. *She is taken.*

YORK.

Joan of Arc, damsel of France,
I have you fast. Where is your God now?
Still, wriggling hag, enchantress, hold your tongue!
Curse all you want when you burn at the stake.

JOAN (*responding to her grasp*).

Lord of York,
You want the grace and power others have.
You crave the crown of England. Lust for it.
It pollutes your thoughts each waking hour,
You are stained with the blood of innocents,
Corrupt and tainted with a thousand vices.

YORK.

What witchcraft is this?

JOAN.

May never glorious sun reflect his beams,
Upon your family and your progeny,
But darkness and the gloomy shade of death,
Environ you, till mischance and despair
Drive you to a savage death.

YORK.

Ay, ay! Away with you to execution!
Never will York be cut down by a maid.

Exit. MARGARET *stubs out her cigarette*.

ACT ONE

Scene One – Ten Years Earlier, Margaret Arrives in England

London. The Palace.

HENRY.
Welcome all from your happy voyage from France.

SUFFOLK.
Your High Imperial Majesty
I have performed my task. And humbly now,
In sight of England and her lordly peers,
Deliver up to you, your Queen.
The happiest gift that ever Marquess gave,
The fairest queen that ever king received.

HENRY.
Suffolk, we thank you. Welcome, Queen Margaret.
I can express no kinder sign of love
Than this kind kiss. O Lord, that lends me life,
Lend me a heart replete with thankfulness!
For you have given me in this beauteous face
A world of earthly blessings to my soul,
If sympathy of love unite our thoughts.

MARGARET *embraces him, a faux pas.*

MARGARET.
Great King of England and my gracious lord,
The mutual conference that my mind hath had,
With you, by day, by night, waking and in my dreams,
In courtly company or at my beads,
Makes me the bolder to salute my king
With ruder terms, such as my wit affords
And over-joy of heart doth minister.

HENRY.
Such is the fullness of my heart's content.
Lords, with one cheerful voice welcome my love.

ALL.
Long live Queen Margaret, England's happiness!

MARGARET (*aside*).
So here the son of Henry Five and there the brother.
And these fellow nobles I will soon embrace.
Such a happy breed.
I thank you all.

SUFFOLK.
My Lord Protector, so it please your grace,
Here are the articles of contracted peace
Between our sovereign and the French King Charles.

GLOUCESTER (*reads*).
'Imprimis, it is agreed between the French
King Charles, and the Marquess of Suffolk,
ambassador for Henry King of England, that
the said Henry shall espouse the Lady Margaret,
daughter unto Reignier King of Naples, Sicilia and
Jerusalem, and crown her Queen of England before the
thirtieth of May next ensuing. Item, that the duchy
of Anjou and the county of Maine shall be released
and delivered to the King her father' –
(*Drops the paper from his hand.*)

HENRY.
Uncle, how now!

GLOUCESTER.
Pardon me, gracious lord,
Some sudden qualm has struck me at the heart
And dimmed my eyes that I can read no further.

HENRY.
Suffolk, I pray, read on.

SUFFOLK (*reads*).
'Item: It is agreed that the duchies of Anjou
and Maine shall be released and delivered over to the King
her father,
and she sent over of the King of England's own
proper cost and charges, without having any dowry.'

HENRY.

They please us well. Lord Marquess,
We here create you the first Duke of Suffolk.
Cousin of York, we here discharge you from being Regent,
In these parts of France, till term of eighteen months.
Thanks, Cousin of York,

MARGARET *flinches*.

thanks, uncle Gloucester,
Somerset, Warwick, and Cardinal too.
We thank you all for the great favour done,
In entertainment to my princely Queen.
Come, let us in, and with all speed provide
To see her coronation be performed.

Exit HENRY, MARGARET *and* SUFFOLK.

GLOUCESTER.

Brave peers of England, pillars of the state,
To you Duke Humphrey must unload his grief,
Your grief, the common grief of all the land.
What? Did my brother Henry spend his youth,
His valour, coin and people, in the wars?
Did he so often lodge in open field,
In winter's cold and summer's parching heat,
To conquer France, his true inheritance?
Have you yourselves, noble Somerset,
Brave York, and victorious Warwick,
Received deep scars in France and Normandy?

They all unroll their sleeves in practised manner.

Or has the reverend Cardinal and myself,
With all the learned council of the realm,
Studied so long, sat in the council-house
Early and late, debating to and fro
How France and Frenchmen might be kept in awe,
And saw His Highness in his infancy
Crowned in Paris despite his foes?
And shall these labours and these honours die?
Shall Henry's conquest, and his vigilance,

Your deeds of war and all our counsel die?
O peers of England, shameful is this league!
Fatal this marriage, cancelling your fame,
Undoing all, as if it had never been!

CARDINAL.

Humphrey, what means this passionate discourse?
Anjou and Maine are minor counties.
France is ours, and will remain ours.

GLOUCESTER.

Ay, your grace, we would keep it if we could,
But now it is impossible we should.
Suffolk, the new-made duke that rules the roost,
Has given the duchies of Anjou and Maine
To the girl's father.

WARWICK.

These counties were the keys of Normandy
I grieve that they are past recovery.
Anjou and Maine! I won them both in battle,
Those provinces these arms of mine did conquer.

YORK.

For Suffolk's dukedom, may he suffocate!
I never read but England's kings have had
Large sums of gold and dowries with their wives.
And our King Henry gives away his own,
To match with her that brings no advantage?

GLOUCESTER (*reads*).

A proper jest, and never heard before,
That Suffolk should demand fifteen per cent
For costs and charges in transporting her!
She should have stayed in France and starved in France.

CARDINAL.

My Lord of Gloucester, now you grow too hot.
It was the pleasure of my lord the King.

GLOUCESTER.

In your face I see your fury. If I stay longer,
We shall begin our ancient bickerings.

Lordings, farewell, and say, when I am gone,
I prophesied France will be lost before long.

Exits.

CARDINAL.
So, there goes our Protector in a rage.
It's known to you he is my enemy,
And no great friend, I fear me, to the King.
Consider, lords, until there is a prince,
Born to this Queen, he is the next by blood,
And heir apparent to the English crown.
What though the common people favour him,
Calling him 'Humphrey, the good Duke of Gloucester',
Clapping their hands, and crying with loud voice,
'God preserve the good Duke Humphrey!'
I fear me, lords, for all this flattering gloss,
He will be found a dangerous Protector.

Exits.

YORK.
Why should he, then, protect our sovereign,
He being of age to govern of himself?

SOMERSET.
Cousin of York, though Humphrey's pride
And greatness of his place be grief to us,
Yet let us watch the haughty Cardinal.
We are both closer to the crown than him.
If Gloucester be displaced, he'll be Protector.

Exits.

WARWICK.
Pride went before, ambition follows him.
Somerset himself has claim to the throne.
While they do labour for their own preferment,
Behoves it us to labour for the realm.
My deeds, my plainness and my housekeeping,
Has won great favour of the common man,
The exploits of my navy, my merchants too
Have kept the traders and the guilds happy.

And, sister York, your acts in Ireland,
In bringing them to civil discipline,
Your late exploits won in the heart of France,
When you brought peace and ended war,
Means you are feared and honoured by the people.
Let's join together, for the public good.
Do what we can, to bridle and suppress
The pride of Suffolk and the Cardinal,
And crush Somerset's ambition.

YORK.

Let's make a show of love to proud Duke Humphrey,
And, when we spy advantage, take our time.
King Henry, surfeiting in joys of love,
With his new bride and England's dear-bought Queen,
Whose bookish rule has pulled this fair realm down,
Will then yield England to my better path.

Scene Two – Queen Margaret Makes Herself at Home

London. The Palace, MARGARET's *chamber.*

Enter MARGARET *and* JOAN. MARGARET *carries a guide to the nobility of England.*

JOAN.

Everything is wet. Your packed robes are wet,
The fog is wet, the king himself is /

MARGARET.

/ Stop Joan, stop. You are not here. I left you back in France.

JOAN.

No. I am here. You are here. Worst of all the English are here. What is that?

MARGARET.

A guide to the noble families of England. I know what I am doing.

JOAN.

Your grandmother would be on page one of such a book in
France. She paid every one of my soldiers. There would be a
picture of your father picking me up and carrying me
wounded from the battlefield. They cursed these Lancaster
men who stole the crown from France, and now you marry
the son of that usurper Henry V.

MARGARET.

The war is over. France is France once more, let England be
England. I am not my grandmother. My heart swells with
pride for what she did for France, but I am Queen of England
now. I am the peace. I will make this treaty work. I will give
myself to my new country.

JOAN.

You nearly drowned in the Channel for this. There are no
vineyards, there is no cheese.

MARGARET.

They have made a friend of their damp and heavy weather. It
protects them.

JOAN.

Pah. They sing of Agincourt, their hero Henry Five. Every
mother of France knows her sons were killed by mud. The
foul English brought their weather with them.

MARGARET.

The war left its residue on all of us. No soldier came home
with his soul untainted. Except you. These families were all
snarling here before I came, ready to catch each other by the
throat.

JOAN.

And now they will turn their hatred all on you. Your
grandmother brought you as a crying babe to my execution.
As the smoke blinded me and my head fell forward, you
were the last sound I heard on this earth. Your infant soul
knew divine justice then. Those nobles, Warwick and York,
were on the platform at my death. They fed the fire with their
Agincourt-scarred hands, desperate for me to die. Your new
husband signed my death warrant.

MARGARET.
He was but a child.

JOAN.
But someone signed his name.

MARGARET *consults her book*.

MARGARET.
Duke Humphrey of Gloucester, the Lord Protector.

JOAN.
Gloucester! So it was him who instructed them to burn my body three times, and have my ashes thrown into the Seine like offal. Take this. (*Places a dagger on the open book*.) It is good and strong to defend yourself. The hilt is good for a woman's hand. It is excellent for giving hard clouts and buffets.

MARGARET.
I don't need it.

JOAN.
You will. Save it for a rainy day, or maybe a snowy one.

MARGARET.
Peace! Peace.

JOAN *re-sheaths knife*.

My King is no warmonger, he is a gentle king who prays for a gentle heir. Though I think no woman has ever been within his chamber. He fumbles towards this marriage like a boy. He is their precious stone set in this savage sea.

JOAN.
Fate and our families threw us together. I didn't choose this restlessness. It was the English who denied me a grave. Help me find my peace.

Scene Three – Margaret Learns the Ways of the English Court

London. The Palace. The petitioners gather.

BAGOT.
Let's stand close.
My Lord Protector will come this way by and by,
And then we may deliver our petitions.

Waves a letter.

HUME (*aside*).
Jesus it is my Lord of Suffolk. He won't like this.

Enter SUFFOLK *and* MARGARET.

BAGOT.
Here he comes, I think, and the new Queen with him.
I'll be the first, sure.

SUFFOLK.
How now, fellow! Would you have anything with me?

BAGOT.
I pray, my Lord Suffolk, pardon me. I took you for my Lord
Protector.

MARGARET (*reads*).
'To my Lord Protector'! Are your petitions to his lordship?
Let me see them.
(*To* HUME.) What is yours?

HUME *doesn't hand it over.*

SUFFOLK.
What's here? Hand it over.

Takes letter from HUME.

'Against the Duke of Suffolk, for enclosing the commons of
Ipswich.'
How now? Do you stand by this?

HUME.

> Alas, sir, I am but a poor petitioner of our whole township.
> We are all commoners, but without a common to graze our
> herd.
> So, yes, I deliver this to you.

MARGARET.

> Let me see? (*Takes letter.*)
> What is your name?

HUME.

> My name is Hume, Majesty.

MARGARET.

> Your penmanship is good.

SUFFOLK.

> What have you?

BAGOT (*giving his petition*).

> Against my master, the armourer Thomas Horner,
> for saying that the Duke of York was rightful heir to the
> crown.

MARGARET.

> What says you? Did the Duke of York say she was rightful
> heir to the crown?

BAGOT.

> No, forsooth, my master said that she was, and that the King
> is an usurper.

SUFFOLK.

> We'll hear more of your treasonable matter before the King.
> (*Keeps letter.*)
> Away base cullions!

MARGARET (*to* HUME).

> Not you. Follow within, when I am ready.

HUME *waits*.

> Is this the fashion in the court of England?
> Is this the government of Britain's isle?
> With letters and listing of grievances
> To the Lord Protector? Who like a sponge

That soaks up the devotion of the people
Does bloat on their love and their loyalty?
How does a king get to know his people?
Shall King Henry be a pupil still?
Under the surly Gloucester's governance?
His people will despise his spineless rule.

SUFFOLK.
Madam, be patient.

MARGARET.
Beside the haughty Protector, have we Somerset, Warwick,
the Cardinal
And grumbling York, and not the least of these
Can do more in England than the King.

SUFFOLK.
And she of these that can do most of all
Cannot do more in England than Warwick.
She is no simple peer.
She surrounds this realm with ships and men-at-arms
She is Lord of Calais, all merchants, sailors
And soldiers know her by name.
The pirates in these waters too.
For I am bold to counsel you in this.
Although Somerset has claim to the throne,
Yet must we join with him for his stability.
Do you as I do in these early days,
Wink at Warwick's insolence,
At York's usurping ambition,
At the Cardinal's pride,
At all the crew of them:
Till they have snared the shepherd of the flock.
Till we have brought proud Gloucester in disgrace.
So, one by one, we'll weed them out at last,
And you yourself could steer this happy helm.

Exits.

MARGARET (*to* HUME).
Am I a queen merely in title and in style,
And must be made a subject to this duke?
I tell you I thought my King would resemble your Henry V,

In courage, courtship and proportion,
But all his mind is bent to holiness,
To number Ave-Maries on his beads.

HUME.

God save the King!

MARGARET.

I would the college of the cardinals
Would choose him Pope, and carry him to Rome.
Why does he not fight for his right to rule?

Enter GLOUCESTER.

GLOUCESTER.

Madam, what have you done with my petitioners?

MARGARET.

Indolent Duke. They tired of the wait.

Scene Four – Margaret Encourages the King to Rule

London. The Palace.

HENRY.

For my part, noble lords, I care not which.
Either Somerset or York, both equals in my sight.

YORK.

If York has ill-demeaned herself in France,
Then let her be denied the Regentship.

SOMERSET.

If Somerset be unworthy of the place,
Let York be Regent. I will yield to her.

WARWICK.

Whether your grace be worthy, maybe, but
Dispute not that York is the worthier.

CARDINAL.

Ambitious Warwick, let your betters speak.

WARWICK.

My grace, you are not my better in the field.

YORK.

Warwick may live to be the best of all.

SOMERSET.

All in this presence are your betters, Warwick.

MARGARET (*aside*).

Two hours later.

WARWICK.

Show some reason, assembled lords
Why Somerset should be preferred in this.

MARGARET.

Because the King, forsooth, will have it so.

GLOUCESTER.

Madam, the King is old enough himself
To give his censure. These are no wifely matters.

MARGARET.

If he be old enough, what needs your grace
To be Protector of his excellence?

GLOUCESTER.

Madam, I am Protector of the realm,
And, at his pleasure, will resign my place.

MARGARET.

Resign it then.

GLOUCESTER.

I say, my sovereign?

HENRY.

–

GLOUCESTER.

Back then to the matter we have in hand,
York is meetest woman to be your regent in the realm of
France.

SUFFOLK.
Before you make election, give me leave
To show some reason, of no little force,
Why York is most unmeet of any woman.

YORK.
I'll tell you, nobles, why I am unmeet.
First, for I cannot flatter you in pride,
Next, if I be appointed for France,
My Lord of Somerset will keep me,
Without revenue or soldiers as he did before.

WARWICK.
That foul act did I witness.

SOMERSET.
Peace, headstrong Warwick!

WARWICK.
Image of pride, why should I hold my peace?

SUFFOLK.
Please it Your Majesty, there is a man,
An apprentice armourer, in service to the Duke of York,

Enter BAGOT, *distressed.*

Does accuse his master of high treason.
The man, who spends every waking hour
Making weapons for the Duke, his words were these:
The Duke of York is rightful heir unto the English crown,
And that Your Majesty is a usurper.

HENRY.
What means this, Suffolk? Tell me what is this?

YORK.
Does anyone accuse York for a traitor?

SUFFOLK.
York's armourer says this, not the Duke of York herself.

HENRY.
Uncle what shall we say to this in law?

GLOUCESTER.

Let the armourer have a day appointed
For single combat against his servant.

BAGOT *faints*.

For the servant has witness of his master's malice
This is the law. As is Duke Humphrey's way.
And, if I may, judge, my lord
Let Somerset be Regent over the French,
Because in York this breeds suspicion.

HENRY *assents*.

SOMERSET.

I humbly thank Your Majesty.

YORK.

I mark this Suffolk.

Enter HUME *with a babe in arms*.

MARGARET.

Stay, Humphrey Duke of Gloucester, before you go,
Give up your staff.
Henry will to himself and his son Protector be,
And God shall be his hope, his stay, and his guide.

HENRY.

Please go in peace, Humphrey, no less beloved
Than when you were Protector to your King.

MARGARET.

God and King Henry govern England's realm.
Give up your staff, sir.

GLOUCESTER.

My staff?
Here, noble Henry, is my staff.
As willingly do I the same resign
As ever your father Henry made it mine,
And even as willingly at your feet I leave it
As others would ambitiously receive it.

Exit all but MARGARET.

MARGARET.

Yes. Now is Henry King, and Margaret Queen,
(*To babe in arms*.) And this angelic boy must now, with
pomp, be seen.

Scene Five – The Queen Administers the Realm

London. The Palace. Toys strewn across the floor.

MARGARET.

Write. To the Mayor of London, argue strongly against the
confiscating of horses from my tenants in Enfield, also to the
monks of Eddingham, full thanks for housing the chorister
who was taken with leprosy, send word to my lieutenant to
arrange for us to leave the city. We will need a carriage. A
small team, only closest men-at-arms.
Where is the money?

HUME.

I did what I could, Majesty. I urged the custom-men of
Dover strictly at your command to pay what they owe. I
spoke words from my heart, praying that they paid up, but to
little effect. They have sent letters, humbly, but no money.

MARGARET (*reads*).

Did you write 'exhort and require you'?

HUME.

Yes. As you said I wrote.
Majesty, it's this dowry tax. It's breeding resentment against
you, madam. They will not pay. They ask 'how many more
years must English men suffer what' forgive me, 'the French
ought to pay.'

MARGARET.

This weave of well-seeming laws laid down by Gloucester
hampers my every move. This dowry tax does damage to the
crown.

HUME.

> Forgive me, Majesty, taxation has been by consent in
> England since the time of King John. We English don't like
> to be 'exhorted'.

MARGARET.

> Where is the Fourme d'Ambert?

HUME.

> All shipments of cheese from France hit foul weather. I have
> some Kentish rennet.

MARGARET.

> That is not cheese. Write.

HUME *writes*.

> Take six quarts of the best stoakings with two quarts of
> cream. Place on the fire till hot, add two quarts of hot water
> and two egg yolks, and one spoonful of sugar, two spoonfuls
> of rennet, mingle all together and do not stop stirring for a
> second. Leave to cool, drain and press, set it in nettle leaves
> and turn daily for three weeks. Take it to the kitchens. Make
> me some cheese.

HUME.

> Yes, ma'am.

MARGARET.

> I haven't finished with you yet. 'To the Sergeant-at-arms,
> Margaret, by the grace of God, Queen of England and of
> France, and Lady of Ireland. Well beloved, et cetera, et
> cetera, our resorting at our castle of Coventry and
> sequestered at the hunting lodge, et cetera, et cetera, we
> desire and pray you that the game be spared. And cherished,
> without suffering any other person to hunt or have shot,
> et cetera, et cetera, till we get there' with our afflicted King.
> I must hunt while he rests.

HUME (*writes then reads*).

> – as we trust, especial thanks, et cetera –

MARGARET.

> Make all arrangements for us to get to the hunting lodge with
> the King, under cover, no one must know he is sick.

HUME.

Before we leave the capital, Majesty, I must share other pressing news. There is unrest, Your Majesty, in Kent. They say the Duke of Somerset fares ill in his governance of France.

MARGARET.

Do Kentishmen haunt me still? They made great swords and bows to kill French men. They were the engine of the war. What is Somerset to them?

HUME.

He has no want of their trades, and since the French wars are ended hardship does ensue.

MARGARET.

Somerset's failings will bring no joy to Kent, though France will be the happier.

HUME.

Majesty, the people are grateful to you. Your diligence on their behalf, for proportioning the rents and protecting the measures and the common lands, and ensuring the gallons of sack flow merrily through the ports. Though I have heard, some tell, there are / rumours –

MARGARET.

/ Get to it.

HUME.

Majesty, the common men are made hard-hearted with their lot. Poverty eats at their souls.

MARGARET.

Hume, your honesty has become the greatest part of you. Be warned. The King prays for his people every day from his bed, while I demean myself pleading for unpaid taxes, and wait and wait on our debts. I have become an adamant woman, a beggar queen. Recession in the hearts of men will hurt his realm. Deliver these presently. We must to the midlands with all discretion.

She takes the rennet. Looks at it. Throws it away.

Scene Six – Margaret Prays for Guidance

London. The Palace Chapel.

HENRY.
　We thank God for the excellent schooling of sweet Edward,
　And the blessing of a praiseworthy schoolmaster.

　They pray.

MARGARET.
　I cannot reach the ecstasy he reaches. Teach me.

JOAN.
　It was something I did not control. The church bells gave me
　peace. When they rang out across the French countryside, I
　knew unity was possible for France.

MARGARET.
　Heaven delights to hear his prayers, while I pluck down
　nothing from the heavens but silence. Prayer refuses me,
　while my mind teems with darkest dreads unbidden. For
　years now the King has not ruled and the corruption-
　concealing chaos breeding in this kingdom will unseat us. If
　God will not help me what do I do? You must teach me.

JOAN.
　I have no skills but holy war.

MARGARET.
　I won't be needing that. The devil knew what he was doing
　when he made man politic. I will look after the merchants of
　this country, the parishes and the universities. The merchants
　pray for profit and I will answer their prayers.

JOAN.
　And let the lords spend themselves in quarrels? You will be
　a target of their spleen if you have no God to protect you.
　Protect the crown, it is divinely given and can only be
　divinely taken away.

MARGARET.
　With what? My wits alone?

HENRY.

Meg, we should prepare for the mass.

MARGARET.

My lord, I need to remain in communion with the Blessed
Virgin. I will follow.

HENRY.

Blessings upon you, Meg.

Exits.

MARGARET.

If you won't help me, go back to France.

JOAN.

I wish I could. This restless eternity is not my choice.

MARGARET.

If Henry does not lead, these nobles cannot follow, and so
they will feast on their own appetites. I must stitch the
tapestry of this kingdom together with knots I pray will hold.

Scene Seven – Margaret Swears an Oath

London. The Parliament.

HENRY.

I muse my Lord of Gloucester is not here.
It's not his wont to be the hindmost man.
Whatever occasion keeps him from us now?

MARGARET.

Our Parliament sits here in full session
These several days without his presence.
Have you not seen? Or will you not observe
The strangeness of his altered countenance?
He knits his brow and shows an angry eye,
And passes by with stiff unbowed knee,
Disdaining duty that to us belongs.

SUFFOLK.
>Gloucester is a man unsounded yet
>And full of cruel deceit.
>Smooth runs the water where the brook is deep.

HENRY.
>My Lord of Suffolk, why press so sharply against the Duke?

YORK.
>Did he not, in his Protectorship,
>Levy great sums of money through the realm
>For soldiers' pay in France, and never sent it?

CARDINAL.
>Tut, these are petty faults to faults unknown.
>Which time must bring to light in smooth
>Duke Humphrey.

HENRY.
>My lords, at once, the care you have of us,
>To mow down thorns that would annoy our foot,
>Is worthy praise, but, shall I speak my conscience?
>Our kinsman Gloucester is as innocent
>From meaning harm to our royal person
>As is the sucking lamb or harmless dove.

Enter SOMERSET.

SOMERSET.
>All health unto my gracious sovereign!

HENRY.
>Welcome, Lord Somerset. What news from France?

SOMERSET.
>That all your interest in those territories
>Is utterly bereft you. All is lost.

HENRY.
>Cold news, Lord Somerset, but God's will be done.

MARGARET.
>This is such unwanted news to our lord.
>We can brook no more hardship in this realm.

YORK.

My God I am a prophet!
York would have fared better as Regent.
Did I not argue vehemently so?

WARWICK.

What news of Calais? What of my garrison there?
(*Aside to* YORK.) I must go. Send word of this day's events.

Exit WARWICK. *Enter* GLOUCESTER.

GLOUCESTER.

Where goes my Lord of Warwick in such haste?
Pardon, my liege, that I am so late.

SUFFOLK.

Nay, Gloucester, know that you have come too soon.

MARGARET (*waving letters*).

The sale of regal appointments in France
If they were known, as the suspect is great,
Would make you quickly hop without your head.

GLOUCESTER.

I came to talk of parliamentary affairs,
(*To* MARGARET.) As for your spiteful false objections,
Prove them!

YORK.

It's thought, my lord, that you took bribes of France,
And, being Protector, stayed the soldiers' pay,
By means whereof His Highness has lost France.
Somerset brings his news this very hour.

SOMERSET.

I have no accusation to make here,
Despite the drift to rancour in this room.

GLOUCESTER (*to* MARGARET).

Who is it that has proof?
I never robbed the soldiers of their pay,
Nor ever had one penny bribe from France.
So help me God, as I have watched the night,
Ay, night by night, in studying good for England,
No, no, no, no, my liege this is not true.
Many a pound of mine own proper store,

Because I would not tax the needy commons,
Have I disbursed to the garrisons,
And never asked for restitution

HENRY.
It serves you well, my lord, to say so much.

GLOUCESTER.
I say no more than truth, so help me God!

SUFFOLK.
I do arrest you of high treason in His Highness' name,
For schemes against the crown,
And here commit you to the Lord Cardinal
To keep, until your further time of trial.

HENRY.
My Lord of Gloucester, it's my special hope
That you will clear yourself from all suspicion,
My conscience tells me you are innocent.

GLOUCESTER.
Ah, gracious lord, these days are dangerous.
Virtue is choked with foul ambition
And charity chased hence by rancour's hand.
I know their plot is to have my life,
And if my death might make this island happy,
And prove the period of their tyranny,
I would expend it with all willingness.
My fate is mere the prologue to their play,
And you, my sovereign lady, with the rest,
Causeless have laid disgraces on my head,
And with your best endeavour have stirred up
My beloved nephew to be my enemy.

MARGARET.
My lord, his railing is intolerable!
He'll numb our ears and hold us here all day.
Lord Cardinal, he is your prisoner.

GLOUCESTER.
Ah! Thus King Henry throws away his crutch
Before his legs are firm to bear his body.
Thus is the shepherd beaten from your side,

And wolves are gnarling who shall gnaw you first.
Ah, that my fear were false! Ah, that it were!
For, good King Henry, your decay I fear.

Exit GLOUCESTER *with* CARDINAL.

HENRY.
My lords, what to your wisdoms seems best,
Do or undo, as if ourself were here.

MARGARET.
What? Will Your Highness leave the Parliament?
We have such urgent matters to attend for France.

HENRY.
Ay, Margaret, do what you will, for France.
My heart is drowned with grief.
Good Somerset, come let us pray for our diminished lands.

Exit HENRY *and* SOMERSET.

MARGARET.
Henry, my lord, is cold in great affairs,
Too full of foolish pity for his uncle.
Believe me, lords, were none more wise than I,
And yet herein I judge mine own wit good,

Re-enter CARDINAL.

This Gloucester should be quickly rid the world,
To rid us of the fear we have of him.

CARDINAL.
That he should die is worthy policy,
But yet we want a reason for his death.
It's best he be condemned in a court of law.

SUFFOLK.
But, to my mind, that is no policy.
The King will labour still to save his life,
The commons loudly rise, to save him too.

YORK.
And yet we have only trivial argument,
Nothing but mistrust, nothing worthy of death.
Say as you think, and speak it from your soul.

SUFFOLK.
>Things are often spoke and seldom meant,
>But in this my heart accords with my tongue.
>To preserve my sovereign from his foe,
>Say but the word, and I will be his priest.

CARDINAL.
>And I'll provide his executioner absolution.
>I tender so the safety of my liege.

SUFFOLK.
>Here is my hand, the deed is worthy doing.

MARGARET.
>And so say I.

YORK.
>And I, and now we three have spoke it.

JOAN (*to* MARGARET).
>You have sworn an oath against God! You have let York hold
>your soul in her hand. She felt it corrupt. She has you now.

>JOAN *disappears. Enter* HUME.

HUME (*aside*).
>My Queen, I have intelligence from Ireland.

MARGARET.
>To all.

HUME.
>Great lords, from Ireland here comes news.
>The rebels there are up and put Englishmen to the sword.
>Our commanders plead for help to stop this skirmish before
>it makes a war,
>They ask that the Parliament responds with all haste.

YORK (*to* MARGARET).
>What counsel give you in this weighty cause?

MARGARET.
>Say, if this Irish spark proves a raging fire,
>Should wind and fuel be sent to feed it up?

YORK.
>What? Do nothing? Nay, then, a shame!

CARDINAL (*to* MARGARET).
Majesty?

MARGARET.
My lords, King Henry prays for no more war.

Unhealthy pause.

CARDINAL.
My Lord of York, try what your fortune is.
The uncivil kerns of Ireland are in arms
And temper clay with blood of Englishmen.
To Ireland you will lead a band of men,
Collected choicely, from each county some,
And try your hap against the Irishmen?

YORK.
I will, my lord, so please His Majesty?

MARGARET.
Does not the King deems it a sin to rush to war?

CARDINAL.
You must in time learn how Parliament works.
Our authority is his consent,
And what we do establish in crisis he confirms.
Then, noble York, take you this task in hand.

YORK.
I am content. Provide me soldiers, lords,
While I take order for mine own affairs.

MARGARET.
Cardinal! I will give the order.

CARDINAL.
Madam.

MARGARET.
This charge, Lord York, Lord Suffolk will perform.

YORK.
My Lord of Suffolk, within fourteen days
At Bristol I expect my soldiers.
From there with Warwick's fleet I'll ship them all for Ireland.

SUFFOLK.
I'll see it truly done, my Lord of York.

CARDINAL (*aside*).
Lord Suffolk, you and I must talk of that other concern.

Exit severally in all directions, leaving MARGARET *and* HUME *apart.*

MARGARET.
Faster than springtime showers,
Comes thought on thought,
And not a thought but thinks on strategy.
No sooner is haughty Gloucester maimed,
Than York's brain, more busy than the labouring
Spider, sets her web. And I am caught.
Well, Margaret, now is it politically done,
To send her packing with a host of men.
It was men she lacked and now we give her them!
We've put sharp weapons in a madwoman's hands.
And this foul tempest shall not cease to rage
Until the golden circuit's on her head.
Why, then from Ireland will she come with strength
To reap the harvest which these times will sow.
For Humphrey being dead, as he shall be,
And Henry lost in grief, what's next for me?

Scene Eight

The docks at Bristol.

HUME.
This muster is a gruff and ugly thing. These six thousand
men are more war-hardened and scar-rattled than any I have
clapped eyes on before. To make up the numbers they broke
open the prisons and poured them into the taverns, and from
there they are rolling onto the ships. God help the Irish when
this lot land.

Do you like my livery? Before I was a scrivener I was a broiderer. I can stitch the crest of many a house. I wear the red rose of the House of Lancaster here. My lady the Queen deigns it so. I also – (*Puts cloak on other shoulder.*) carry the white rose of the House of York here. Lancaster. York. Lancaster. York. You lot on my right see me one way. You lot on my left see me another. You behind me have no fucking clue, and you in front of me know what a dirty little turncoat I can be. But there is method in my madness. I carry letters to all the peoples of this realm. These letters are full of Her Majesty's nervous entreaties:

'How much wine have you imported for August?'
'How many banquets have the guild of fishmongers' held?'
'What duty on the shipments of wool to Flanders?'
In these answers she reads the ebb and flow of her realm, the readiness of her nobles and the loyalty of her people.

And sometimes I need to know what lies behind other seals. I have one letter here to a man of Kent from a lord of York. As a loyal subject of Her Majesty there is only one action I can here perform. (*Snaps a letter open, reads.*) Oh dear. Oh Lordy.

Here I find a letter to one Jack Cade of Kent. I have heard of him. He's that famous fighter. (*Reads.*) 'Stir up this England into some black storm. Blow ten thousand souls to heaven or hell.' Oh shit. 'Stir up this England into some black storm. Blow ten thousand souls to heaven or hell. Make commotion, as full well as you can.' To unleash him here, in England? – (*Makes the sign of the cross.*) is reckless.

There is a story every child knows; he fought so long in battle his thighs were stabbed with so many daggers yet he danced like a happy porpentine.

(*Reads again.*) 'You now shall be my devil. Address the people's poverty but slyly, make them question the King's authority. Make them think he cares not to mend their hardships. By this I shall perceive the commons' mind, how they affect the house and claim of York. I know no pain the King can inflict upon you. Even if you be taken, racked and tortured. Nothing will make you say York moved you to this

rebellion. Then from Ireland will I come with my strength
and reap the harvest which you now will sow.'

What do I do with this? If it is not delivered York will know.
If it is delivered to Jack Cade what happens then? Sometimes
I wish I didn't meddle.

Scene Nine – Margaret Examines Her Conscience

London. The Palace Chapel.

MARGARET *kneels,* JOAN *stands, off.*

MARGARET.
Pray, show yourself that I may seek your counsel. I have
sworn an oath to kill the King's uncle. My husband, my
father and my beloved grandmother would damn me for it. If
they knew. You know.

Nothing. She stands. Sees JOAN.

O hold me not with silence over long.

I would trade these – (*Holds beads.*) for the knife you once
offered me. The demon who cut you down is stalking the
crown. I need her support yet fear her ambition. My beads
are worn with supplications for your counsel. Help me now.
I cannot find the path without you.

JOAN *remains silent.*

You brandished a holy sword. Where is it now? I find no
help in pretty numbered beads. You lived in virtue, you died
with honour. This course I choose is expedient. Tell me how
does this oath diminish me if it is in support of my husband?
Help me, I beg you.

JOAN *leaves.* MARGARET *throws away her beads.*

This course is set. I must steer as best I can. Abandoned by
you, am I abandoned by God?

Scene Ten – Margaret Loses Her Closest Ally

Bury St Edmunds. A courthouse with a public gallery.

MARGARET.
  You bloody fool!

SUFFOLK.
  I did as I was instructed.

MARGARET.
  This was not the manner of the deed!
  His death was to be somehow a quiet thing,
  Some guilty palsy caused by his disgrace.
  But now! His face is black and full of blood,
  His eyeballs further out than when he lived,
  Staring full ghastly like a strangled man.
  It cannot be but he was murdered here.
  The commons anticipated a trial,
  With good Duke Humphrey's innocence assured.
  What do we do now, my Lord of Suffolk?

SUFFOLK.
  They are coming straight. This will now be known.

  Enter HENRY*,* SOMERSET *and* CARDINAL.

HENRY.
  Go, call our uncle to our presence straight.
  Say we intend to try his grace today.

SUFFOLK.
  I'll call him presently, my noble lord.

  Exits.

HENRY.
  Let the commons in. Open the public gallery.
  Let us hear the evidence against Gloucester.

MARGARET.
  Pray God we may acquit him of suspicion!

HENRY.
  I thank you, Meg. These words content me much.

Re-enter SUFFOLK.

Where is our uncle? What's the matter, Suffolk?

SUFFOLK.
Dead in his chair, my lord. Gloucester is dead.

MARGARET.
Marry, God forbid! Lock the commons out!

HENRY *falters*.

How fares my lord? Help, lords!

SOMERSET.
Rear up his body, wring him by the nose.

MARGARET.
O Henry, open your eyes!

SOMERSET.
He does revive again, madam, be patient.

HENRY.
O heavenly God!

MARGARET.
How fares my gracious lord?

CARDINAL.
Comfort, my sovereign! Gracious Henry, comfort!

HENRY.
Ah, woe is me for Gloucester. God help me now.

Enter WARWICK, *noises off, the commoners assemble outside*.

WARWICK.
It is rumoured, mighty sovereign,
That good Duke Humphrey is traitorously murdered
By Suffolk and the Cardinal's men.
The commons, like an angry hive of bees
That want their leader, scatter up and down
And care not who they sting in this revenge.
I have calmed their spleenful mutiny for now,
Until they hear the manner of his death.

HENRY.

That he is dead, good Warwick, it's too true,
But how he died God knows, not Henry.

WARWICK.

Stay, Somerset, calm the rude multitude till I return.

Exits.

SOMERSET *guards the door from within*.

HENRY.

I fear some violent hands were laid on Humphrey's life.
If my suspicion be false, forgive me, God,
For judgement only does belong to you.

Re-enter WARWICK.

WARWICK.

Gracious sovereign, I did view this body.
Humphrey is murdered.

HENRY.

That is to see how deep my grave is made,
For with his soul flees all my worldly solace,
For now I see my life in death.

SUFFOLK.

What instance gives Lord Warwick for her vow?

WARWICK.

Who finds the heifer dead and bleeding fresh
And sees fast by a butcher with an axe?

MARGARET.

Are you the butcher, Suffolk? Where's your knife?

SUFFOLK.

I wear no knife to slaughter sleeping men.
Say, if you dare, proud Lord of Warwickshire,
That I am at fault in Duke Humphrey's death.

CARDINAL *walks away, disowning* SUFFOLK.

WARWICK.

Madam, be still, with reverent care I say
For every word you might speak on his behalf
Is slander to your royal dignity.

SOMERSET *re-enters*.

SOMERSET.
Dread lord, the commons send you word by me,
Unless Lord Suffolk straight be done to death,
Or banished fair England's territories,
They will by violence tear him from your palace
And torture him with grievous lingering death.
They say, by him the good Duke Humphrey died.
They say, in him they fear Your Highness' death,
And mere instinct of love and loyalty,
Makes them forward in this demand for banishment.

COMMONS (*noises off*).
An answer from the King, my Lord of Somerset!

MARGARET.
My lord, show how quaint an orator you are.
Calm them, gentle King, with your sweet orations.
Stand down the court. We will send an answer presently.

COMMONS (*noises off*).
An answer from the King, or we will all break in!

MARGARET.
Go, Somerset, and tell them all from Henry:
'I thank them for their tender loving care – '

HENRY.
– For, sure, my thoughts do hourly prophesy
Mischance unto my state by Suffolk's hands,
And therefore, by His Majesty I swear,
Whose far unworthy deputy I am,
Suffolk shall not breathe infection in this air
But three days longer, on the pain of death.

Exit SOMERSET. SUFFOLK *crumples to the ground*.

That I have just sworn, makes it irrevocable.
If, after three days' space, you are found here
On any ground that I am ruler of,
The world shall not be ransom for your life.
Come, Warwick, come, good Cardinal go with me,
We'll pray for the soul of gentle Humphrey.

WARWICK.
Cardinal, you must need now prepare a funeral.

CARDINAL *exits separately.*

Exit WARWICK *and* HENRY.

MARGARET.
Suffolk, get you hence.
If you're found near me, you are but dead.

SUFFOLK.
If I depart from you, I cannot live.
To die by you, the privilege were mine,
But from you to die were torture more than death.
O, let me stay, befall what may befall!

Enter HUME.

MARGARET (*to* HUME).
Away!
To France, sweet Suffolk. Let me hear from you.
For wheresoever you are in this world's globe,
I'll have an iris that shall seek you out.

SUFFOLK.
I go.

MARGARET.
And take my courage with thee.

Exit SUFFOLK.

HUME.
Majesty, the Cardinal is dead. He found himself amidst an
angry crowd, and was taken with a sickness that made him
gasp and catch the air, and deny that he was to blame. Some
madness made him blaspheme God and curse men on earth,
revealing the secrets of his overcharged soul. The
commoners cheered that his corruption was palpable and
returned with bloodied keepsakes to their homes.

MARGARET.
Great guilt speaks in this.
I will go tell the heavy message to the King.

Scene Eleven

The dockside at Rye.

Enter HUME *carrying a bloodied sack. Sound of ship's bells and fog horns.*

HUME.
    She asked me for good news of his safe passage to France
    but… a pirate gave me this strange treasure. (*Looks inside
    sack.*) Errghhh!

    Trading Suffolk for the commons' anger could never subdue
    them. This is sport now. The pirate captain was so frighted
    by the anarchy onshore he sliced poor Suffolk's head and
    threw the cargo here to me. I'm scared too. There is a
    giddiness in the air. The people of Kent are marching on
    London, up in arms, and I don't blame them.

    Rips down bulletin from a post.

    Here is Jack Cade's rebellion writ large.
    (*Reads.*) 'Grievance number one: the people are destroyed
    with poverty, the King himself is so poor he may not pay his
    meat nor drink.' That's true.
    All the balladeers of England sing – (*Sings.*) 'He owes more
    crowns than any King of England ought.' I like that tune. 'He
    owes more crowns than any King of England ought.'

    (*Reads.*) 'Grievance number five: the Prince Edward is a
    bastard. His father is the Duke of Suffolk.' Nah, not true.

    (*Reads.*) 'Grievance eight: all the realm of England to be
    held in common.' I agree. I completely agree.

    (*Reads.*) 'Grievance ten: we, his true commons, desire that
    the King, by humble behest, take about his noble person, the
    Duke of York, the true blood, rightful heir of this land.
    Signed, Jack Cade.'

    Fuck me. It should be signed the Duke of York, safe in
    Ireland. (*Rips down bulletins and scrunches them into balls.*)
    Don't stir up souls that already are full pent with sorrow. For
    what? Ambition? Just govern England and feed the people!

We English are sick of this ancient grudge. (*Sets out balls of paper in a line with one gap*.) If you go back beyond Edward III, it goes father, son, father, son, father, grandson! If the crown skips a generation civil strife ensues. Always. Think about it. The generation of brothers that get skipped over burn with bitterness forever. York descends from the third skipped-over brother, the King from the fourth brother. Who gives a fig?

This – (*Holds up sack*.) is all that is left of my Lord of Suffolk. Darkness is descending on my mistress's household. It will be my most gruesome delivery yet.

Exits, singing.

Scene Twelve – The Cade Rebellion

London. The Palace.

MARGARET *with the bloodied sack*. HUME *remains apart*.

MARGARET (*falters*).
    Why was banishment not enough? Why death?
    Often have I heard that grief softens the mind,
    And makes it fearful and degenerate.
    Think therefore on revenge and refuse to weep.

    What answer makes Your Grace to the rebels' demands?

HENRY.
    I will not send soldiers into the city.
    For God forbid so many simple souls
    Should perish by the sword! And I myself,
    Will parley with Jack Cade their general.

MARGARET (*aside*).
    You think you can blow out the raging fire
    With such a weak and feeble breath as this?
    York did not strike this spark of discontent,
    But she has kindled well the flame.
    Her lust for Henry's crown burns in this strife,

And Cade's her devil, make no mistake.
These inky wind-torn bulletins of lies
Laugh at the graver promises that kings must make.

HENRY.
How now, madam!
Still lamenting and mourning for Suffolk's death?

Enter SOMERSET.

SOMERSET.
Madam, the rebels are in Southwark!
Jack Cade calls Your Grace usurper openly.
His army declares all scholars, lawyers, courtiers, gentlemen,
False caterpillars, and intend their deaths.

HENRY.
O graceless men! They know not what they do.

Enter CLIFFORD.

CLIFFORD.
Jack Cade has taken London Bridge.
The citizens fly and jointly swear
To spoil the city and your royal court.

MARGARET.
Somerset, Clifford, take men and quell these rebels.

HENRY.
No, Margaret! God, our hope, will succour us.

MARGARET.
No, my gracious lord. Brave warrior Clifford,
And wily Somerset will save this day.
Go both and chase Jack Cade back down to hell.
Take men and clear the bridge. Go well.
Protect the Prince. Steel the court with guards.

Exit all but HUME.

HUME.
They are turning the city upside down.
Oh my God, it is so exciting out there!
I could not calm myself if I tried.
If England's a common treasury, I'm in.

Scene Thirteen

London. A street in disarray.

Shouts heard from riots all around.

HUME.
　　All food and drink on Jack's score! We have loosed the bolts
　　of our existence and London is a carnival!

REBEL.
　　Let's kill all the lawyers! Throw them in the Thames!

HUME (*trying to wipe ink from her hands*).
　　Jack Cade is making chaos of the capital and I have made
　　a foolish wager with my life. If I can't get this ink off my
　　hands I am dead. I saw a clerk dragged along behind Cade's
　　horse. Anyone who has an education is being killed. The piss
　　conduit in the street now runs with blood. The people are in
　　thrall but no one knows which way to run. I have become a
　　target in this rout.

Elsewhere in the capital:

HENRY.
　　Meg, is Cade come for me?

MARGARET.
　　No, no my lord. You are safe, our guard stand strong and
　　protect us well.
　　Somerset and Clifford are come to comfort you with news.

SOMERSET.
　　My lord, we'll soon have this riot under control.

CLIFFORD.
　　London Bridge is blocked with the bodies of those who flee.
　　Fear grips the city and rout is certain.

HENRY.
　　But in the rout most innocents will be slaughtered as they
　　flee!

MARGARET (*to* CLIFFORD).
　　Oh that I was riding in this broil to crush the traitor Cade.

CLIFFORD.
Your soldiers will quell this riot, Majesty. Stay with the
King.

MARGARET.
Tell the people we will pardon their foolish ardour for Jack
Cade.

Elsewhere in the capital:

HUME.
Houses are emptying, children scream and are trampled.
They have hung a blacksmith over his own forge. Rebels are
being slaughtered in front of their children. The Queen's men
match rebellion with savagery. I see men grief-shot, bereft of
kin. Men's drunken ears prick up to the Queen's promise of a
pardon, and listen and awake from their madness and cry:
'God save the King!'

Elsewhere in the capital:

MARGARET.
Is the traitor Cade in retreat?

CLIFFORD.
He is fled, captured and killed, thank God, and all of his
powers do yield.

HENRY.
Then heaven set open your everlasting gates
To entertain my vows of praise and thanks.

MARGARET.
You're welcome, my lord.

Elsewhere in the capital, dawn approaches:

HUME.
Was ever feather so lightly blown to and fro as this
multitude? Dawn is come and London ruined. Does the
stout-hearted Duke of York know what she has unleashed
upon this land? The fits and stirs of the common heart have
been bridled by her and ridden, to our destruction, and to her
advantage. And what a ruthless thing is this in her. She has
no care but private ambition, while we commoners of

England are toyed with and destroyed. And so the day is lost
and I must save myself.

Elsewhere in the capital, dawn breaks:

SOMERSET.
Madam,
Further to Your Graces, it is now reported
That the Duke of York is newly come from Ireland,
And with a puissant and a mighty power
Of gallow-glasses and stout kerns
Is marching London-bound in proud array.

MARGARET.
In England? By what fleet? What admiral gave that order?

CLIFFORD.
It is rumoured by Warwick's fleet.

SOMERSET.
But still, York proclaims as she comes along,
Her arms are only to remove from you,
Me, the Duke of Somerset, whom she terms traitor.

MARGARET.
Here stands our state betwixt Cade and York distressed.
This is her way. This is her gross conceit.
I pray you, Clifford, ride tomorrow to meet her.
And ask her what's the reason of this show of arms?
Tell her we will send Somerset to the Tower.
And Somerset, we'll commit you there,
Until York's army be dismissed from her.
My lord?

HENRY *assents*.

Go to. We'll hear her out.

Scene Fourteen – Margaret's Parley with York

South of St Albans. A clearing near YORK*'s encampment.*

YORK (*aside*).
> From Ireland now comes York to claim her throne,
> And pluck the crown from feeble Henry's head.
> Raise banners high, burn bonfires bright,
> Sacred soil of England, you will be mine this day.

> *Enter* CLIFFORD.

> Clifford, wolfcub at heel, I accept your greeting.
> Are you a messenger, or come of pleasure?

CLIFFORD.
> A messenger from Henry, our dread liege,
> To know the reason of this army in peace?

YORK (*aside*).
> Scarce can I speak, my choler is so great.
> O, I could hew up rocks and fight with flint,
> I am far better born than is the King,
> More like a king, more kingly in my thoughts,
> But I must make fair weather yet a while,
> Till Henry be more weak and I more strong.

> Clifford, the cause why I have brought this army here
> Is to remove proud Somerset from the King.
> Now as I hear, dearest Gloucester is deceased,
> I know not how, but by some dark corruption.
> So Somerset will try the King for his crown.
> This is seditious to his grace and to the state.

CLIFFORD.
> That is too much presumption on your part.
> But if your arms be to no other end,
> The King has yielded unto your demand.
> The Duke of Somerset is in the Tower.

YORK.
> Upon your honour, is he prisoner?

CLIFFORD.
Upon mine honour, he is prisoner.

YORK.
Then, Clifford, I do dismiss my powers.
(*To troops*.) Soldiers, I thank you all. Disperse yourselves.
Meet me tomorrow in St George's field.
You shall have pay and everything you wish.
(*To* CLIFFORD.) And let my sovereign, virtuous Henry,
Receive all lands, goods, horse, armour, anything I have,
Is his to use /

CLIFFORD.
York, I commend this kind submission.

YORK.
/ so Somerset may die.

Enter HENRY *and* MARGARET *with* PRINCE EDWARD.

MARGARET.
Clifford, does York intend no harm to us?

YORK.
In all submission and humility
York does present herself unto Your Highness.

HENRY.
Then what intends those forces you did bring?

YORK.
To heave the traitor Somerset from hence,
And fight against that monstrous rebel Cade.

MARGARET.
Who, since you set sail, is long defeated.
Your plan to conjure up rebellion,
To summon forth your satanic liegeman,
Has failed. Your plan, and all ambition, are stillborn.

Enter SOMERSET.

HENRY (*aside*).
See, Clifford, Somerset comes plain this way.
Go, bid him hide himself quickly from the duke.

MARGARET.
For thousand Yorks he shall not hide his head,
But boldly stand and front her to her face.

YORK.
How now! Is Somerset at liberty?
(*To* MARGARET.) False Queen!
Your Highness, why have you broken faith with me,
Knowing how hardly I can brook the sight?
King did I call you? No, you are not king.

PRINCE EDWARD.
You are not a king! Kneel to my father!

YORK.
That head of his does not become a crown.
That gold must round engirt these brows of mine,
Here is a hand to hold a sceptre up
And with the same to act controlling laws.

MARGARET.
Never. As I live.

YORK.
Give place. By heaven, you shall rule no more
Over him whom heaven created for your ruler.

SOMERSET.
O monstrous traitor! I arrest you, York,
Of capital treason against the King and crown.

YORK.
I will call in my eldest son to be my bail.
Edward! See here he comes.
I'll warrant he'll make it good.

Enter EDWARD.

MARGARET.
Clifford! Come forward,
Please say if that the bastard boy of York.
Is worth the bail for his traitor mother?

YORK.
O blood-besotted outcast of Anjou,
Your corrupt soul taints every word you speak!

The son of York, your better in his birth,
Shall be his mother's bail, and bane to those
That for my surety will refuse the boy!

MARGARET.
But here is the law. Clifford, deny her bail.
She is arrested, but will not obey.
She offers her eldest son in her stead.

YORK.
Will you not stand surety for me, son?

EDWARD.
Ay, noble mother, if my word will serve.
And if words will not, then my weapon shall.

CLIFFORD.
Why, what a brace of traitors have we here!

YORK.
Look in your glass and call your image so.
I am your king, and you a false-heart traitor.

Enter WARWICK, JOAN *somewhere close.*

MARGARET.
So, it was your fleet that sailed the Irish Sea?
Is this reason enough to stray from Calais?

HENRY.
O, where is faith? O, where is loyalty?
For shame! In duty, bend your knee to me.

MARGARET.
Why, Warwick, has your knee forgot to bow?

WARWICK.
My lord, I have considered with myself
The title of this most renowned duke.
And in my conscience do accept her grace
The rightful heir to England's royal seat.

HENRY.
Have you not sworn allegiance unto me?

WARWICK.
I have.

HENRY.
Can you dispense with heaven for such an oath?

WARWICK.
It is great sin to swear unto a sin,
But greater sin to keep.

MARGARET.
Clifford, Somerset, arm yourselves.

YORK.
Call on Somerset, and all the friends he has,
I am resolved for death or dignity.

CLIFFORD.
The first I hope to grant you, if dreams prove true.

WARWICK.
You were best to go to bed and dream again,
To keep you from the tempest of the field.

MARGARET.
We are resolved to bear a greater storm
Than any you can conjure up today.

CLIFFORD.
And so to arms, victorious liege,
To quell this usurper and her complices.

EDWARD.
Fie! Charity, for shame! Speak not in spite,
For you shall sup with Jesus Christ tonight.

MARGARET.
Foul traitor, that's more than you can tell.

EDWARD.
If not in heaven, you'll surely sup in hell.

Exit all. MARGARET *remains with* HENRY, EDWARD
and, somewhere, JOAN.

MARGARET (*aside*).
Surely now, Joan, you can forgive my oath.
And cleanse my soul of the corruption there?

Not all the water in the rough rude sea,
Can wash off the balm from an anointed king.

JOAN *offers her the dagger,* MARGARET *takes it.*

I am ready to fight this righteous battle.
Devil of York, I come!

End of Act One.

ACT TWO

Scene Fifteen – The Battle of St Albans

St Albans. North of London.

Sounds of battle. HENRY *sits under a tree in the market square.*
MARGARET *cannot reach him.*

MARGARET.
What savage slaughter falls upon these boys?
The fatal strokes that mothers never see,
And yet this fight is but an hour old.
Oh pity! There sits the King of England.
With ranks of boys around him falling dead.

CLIFFORD.
Majesty, help me. Rage is eating me alive.
My father has been killed by York.
I must grind her into the clay of England.

MARGARET.
Wait. There will be a time for fierce redress.

CLIFFORD.
Forgive me. This day is dark before noon.

MARGARET.
This does not end here. The York revenge has been exacted.
Outside the castle alehouse in the mud.
Somerset is dead.
Now only we stand between York and the crown.

CLIFFORD.
She has broken through the fosse and ditches.

MARGARET.
Block them in the lanes but do not kettle.
Trapped men fight on with ever stronger rage.
Keep them in two minds, tempt them to fly,
Keep the rout so vivid they can taste it.

CLIFFORD.
Majesty, these narrow lanes are barely two spans wide
Our men are piling one atop another
With barely room enough to fall down dead.

MARGARET.
But our sovereign?
Look see, he sits alone beneath the oak tree's shade,
While arrows rend the hearts of boys who guard him.

CLIFFORD.
For shame, for shame! We must cut through to him.

Another part of the town:

HENRY.
They are coming through the gardens.
The marketplace is strewn about with bodies,
The Abbey doors shut firmly on the dead.
This morning's fight will last just one more hour.
And then I can be a shepherd, not a king.

CLIFFORD *and* MARGARET *reach* HENRY.

MARGARET.
What are you made of? For shame, for shame, away.

HENRY.
Can we outrun the heavens? Good Margaret, stay.

MARGARET.
You'll neither fight, nor fly?

Distant shouts.

If you be taken, we shall see the bottom
Of all of our fortunes. But if we happily escape,
As well we may, we shall to London get.
And where this breach in our fortunes made
May readily be stopped.

HENRY.
Are our men on the rout? Oh confusion.

CLIFFORD.
This is a coward's path. We will live,
But see their day concluded with glory.

MARGARET.
> St Albans battle won by famous York! She will craft the
> legend of this day. It is fifty years since any English lord has
> spilt another's blood in battle. How did it come to this?
>
> To London, all. I must in haste call Parliament to unsnarl this
> bloody day.

Scene Sixteen – Margaret Defies the King

London. Westminster Hall. An empty throne room.

WARWICK.
> I wonder how the King escaped our hands.

YORK.
> While we pursued his horsemen to the north,
> He slyly stole away back to the capital.

RICHARD (*throws down* SOMERSET*'s head*).
> Speak you for me and tell them what I did.

YORK.
> Richard has best deserved of all my sons.

EDWARD.
> But is Your Grace dead, my Lord of Somerset?

RICHARD.
> Thus do I hope to shake King Henry's head.

WARWICK.
> This is the palace of the fearful King,
> And this the regal seat; possess it, York.
> For this is thine and not King Henry's heirs'.

She sits.

> And when the King comes, offer no violence,
> Unless he seeks to thrust you out by force.

YORK.

> The Queen has called an urgent Parliament.
> She little thinks we'll be at her council.
> By words or blows we'll win today our right.

Enter HENRY, *with* CLIFFORD.

CLIFFORD (*aside*).

> My lord, look where the sturdy rebel sits,
> Even in the chair of state. Belike she means,
> To aspire unto the crown and reign as King.
> What? Shall we suffer this? Let's pluck her down!

HENRY (*aside*).

> Be patient, gentle lord.
> Know you not the city still favours them?
> And they have troops of soldiers at their beck?

CLIFFORD (*aside*).

> But when the duke is slain, they'll quickly fly.

HENRY (*aside*).

> Far be the thought of this from Henry's heart,
> To make a shambles of the Parliament house!
> You factious Duke of York, descend my throne,
> And kneel for grace and mercy at my feet.
> I am your sovereign.

YORK.

> I am yours.

CLIFFORD.

> For shame, get down. He made you Duke of York.

YORK.

> It was my inheritance!

CLIFFORD.

> You are a traitor to the crown.

RICHARD.

> Clifford, you are a traitor to the crown
> In following this usurping Henry.

CLIFFORD.

> Whom should I follow but my natural King?

WARWICK.
True, Clifford, and that's the Duke of York.

HENRY.
And shall I stand, and you sit in my throne?

YORK.
It must and shall be so. Content yourself.

WARWICK.
Be Duke of Lancaster. Let York be King.

CLIFFORD.
He is both King and Duke of Lancaster.
And that the Queen of England shall maintain.

WARWICK.
And Warwick shall disprove it. You forget
That we are those which chased you from the field.

YORK.
And slew your father, and with banners flying,
Marched through the city to these palace gates.

EDWARD.
I was there to witness the fatal blow.

CLIFFORD.
Duke of York, of you and these your sons,
Your kinsman and your friends, I'll have more lives
Than drops of blood are in my mother's veins.

YORK.
Please stop denying that I have a greater claim.
Or else, our swords shall plead it in the field.

HENRY.
What title have you, traitor, to the crown?
Your father was, as you art, Duke of York;
I am the son of Henry the Fifth,
Who made the French stoop for mercy,
And seized upon their towns and provinces.

WARWICK.
Talk not of France, since you have lost it all.

HENRY.

The Lord Protector lost it, and not I.
When I was crowned I was but nine months old.

RICHARD.

You are old enough now, and yet, methinks, you lose.
Mother, tear the crown from the usurper's head.

EDWARD.

Sweet Mother, do so. Set it on your head.

YORK.

Sons, peace!

HENRY.

Peace, York! And give King Henry leave to speak.

WARWICK.

My lord, Henry shall speak first. Hear him, lords.
And be you silent and attentive too,
For he that interrupts him shall not live.

HENRY.

Thinks you that I will leave my kingly throne,
Wherein my grandsire and my father sat?
No, first shall war unpeople this my realm.
Our banners, often flown in France,
Are now blood-soaked in England,
To my heart's great sorrow.
My title's good, and better far than hers.

WARWICK.

Prove it, Henry, and you shalt be King.

HENRY.

Henry the Fourth by conquest got the crown.

YORK.

It was by rebellion against his King.

HENRY (*to* CLIFFORD).

I know not what to say. My title's weak.
She is from the third son, I from the fourth.
Is Meg in session with the Parliament?
Tell me, may not a king adopt an heir?

YORK.
What then?

HENRY.
And if he may, then am I lawful King!
For Richard Second, in the view of many lords,
Resigned the crown to Henry the Fourth,
Whose heir my father was, and I am his.

YORK.
He rose against him, being his sovereign,
And made him to resign his crown by force.

WARWICK.
Suppose, my lords, he did it unconstrained,
Think you it were prejudicial to his crown?
For he could not so resign his crown
But that the next heir should succeed and reign.

HENRY (*to* CLIFFORD).
All will revolt from me, and turn to her.

CLIFFORD.
King Henry, be your title right or wrong,
Lord Clifford vows to fight in your defence.
May that ground gape and swallow me alive,
Where I shall kneel to her that slew my father!

HENRY.
O Clifford, how your words revive my heart!

YORK.
Henry of Lancaster, resign your crown.

WARWICK.
Do right unto this princely Duke of York,
Or I will fill the house with armed men.

HENRY.
My Lord of Warwick, hear me but one word.
Let me for this my lifetime reign as King.

YORK.
Confirm the crown to me and to mine heirs,
And you shall reign in quiet while you live.

HENRY.
I am content.
Duke of York, enjoy the kingdom after my decease.

CLIFFORD.
What wrong is this unto the prince, your son!

WARWICK.
What good this is to England and herself!

CLIFFORD.
Base, fearful and despairing Henry!
How have you injured both yourself and us!
Farewell, faint-hearted and degenerate King,
In whose cold blood no spark of honour bides.
I will at once report this foul injustice.

Exit CLIFFORD.

HENRY.
Oh, Meg.

WARWICK.
Why should you sigh, my lord?

HENRY.
Not for myself, Lord Warwick, but my son,
Whom I unnaturally shall disinherit.
But be it as it may. I here resign
The crown to you and to your heirs forever.
Conditionally, that here you take an oath
To cease this civil war, and, whilst I live,
To honour me as your King and sovereign,
And neither by treason nor hostility
To seek to put me down and reign yourself.

YORK.
This oath I willingly take and will perform.

WARWICK.
Long live King Henry!

HENRY.
And long live you and these your forward sons!

YORK.
> Now York and Lancaster are reconciled
> Accursed be he that seeks to make them foes!
> Farewell, my gracious lord. I'll to my castle in Yorkshire.

WARWICK.
> And I'll keep London with my soldiers.

Exit YORK, EDWARD, RICHARD *and* WARWICK

HENRY.
> And I, with grief and sorrow, to the court.

> *Enter* MARGARET *and* PRINCE EDWARD, *followed by*
> CLIFFORD. JOAN *appears.*

> Here comes the Queen, whose arrival betrays her anger.

> *Walks away.*

MARGARET.
> Nay, go not from me. I will follow you.

HENRY.
> Be patient, gentle Queen, and I will stay.

MARGARET.
> Who can be patient in such extremes?
> Ah, wretched man. Would I had died a maid
> And never seen you, never borne you son,
> Seeing you have proved so unnatural a father
> Has he deserved to lose his birthright thus?
> Had you but loved him half so well as I,
> Or felt that pain which I did for him once,
> Or nourished him as I did with my blood,
> You would have left your dearest heart-blood there,
> Rather than have that savage duke your heir
> And disinherited your only son.

JOAN (*to* MARGARET).
> Only God can disinherit a prince!
> This is the crime committed against the French crown.
> The unleashed rage blew England out of France.
> God demands you protect his birthright.
> All power of heaven is now behind you!

PRINCE EDWARD.

Father, you cannot disinherit me.
If you be King, why should not I succeed?

HENRY.

Pardon me, Margaret. Pardon me, sweet son.
The Earl of Warwick and the Duke enforced me.

MARGARET.

Enforced you? Are you King, and will be forced?
I shame to hear you speak. Ah, timorous wretch!
You have undone yourself, your son and me.
And given unto the House of York such head
As you shall reign but by their sufferance.
To entail her and her heirs unto the crown,
What is it, but to make your sepulchre
And creep into it far before your time?
Had I been there, which am a silly woman,
The soldiers should have tossed me on their pikes
Before I would have granted to that act.
But you prefer your life before your honour,
And seeing you do this, I here divorce myself
Both from your table, Henry, and your bed,
Until that Act of Parliament be repealed
Whereby my son is disinherited.
The northern lords that have forsworn their colours
Will follow mine, if once they see them spread.
And spread they shall be, to your foul disgrace,
And utter ruin of the House of York.
Thus do I leave you. Come, son, come Clifford.
Our army is ready. Come, we'll after them.

HENRY.

Stay, gentle Margaret, and hear me speak.

MARGARET.

You have spoke too much already. Get away from me.

HENRY.

Gentle son Edward, you will stay with me?

PRINCE EDWARD.

When I return with victory from the field
I'll see Your Grace. Till then I'll follow her.

MARGARET.
We may not linger thus, to be seized and
Murdered by his enemies. Come, son, away.

Scene Seventeen

Lincolnshire. A country road.

Enter HUME *in rotten battledress.*

HUME.
I wonder how my lady fares at the centre of this storm? I was
her common sense, now she has none.

Here in Lincolnshire, there are tented cities on every plain.
Five thousand horses being shod by smiths. And lines of
carts that snake for miles with food and drink, and guns.
Some men love the King so much they'll sell their pasture to
buy a horse, and follow his cause. Not me. I offered myself
as the muster clerk to be the one who writes every name in
the book bar one. But pish! Here I am tied into this rotten
armour. If I could unbuckle myself and slip into the woods I
would. I am not a soldier. Who wants to thrust a pike in this
mad war, for either side? York proclaimed St Albans such a
fight, that things were settled for a generation. But now
things slide so fast. She grafted ancient quarrels on to the
sacred oak of England, whose deep, deep roots, and boughs
mossed with age, are now diseased, and must we now hew
down and fell all that we love? This misrule makes a
mockery of us all. We are roughshod, ragged, and confused.
I certainly am.

I don't even know whose army this is.

Scene Eighteen – The Battle of Wakefield

Yorkshire. Sandal Castle.

RICHARD.
  Brother, though I be younger, give me leave.

EDWARD.
  No, I can better play the orator.

RUTLAND.
  All talk of war is against Mother's wishes.

RICHARD.
  Little brother, I have reasons strong and forcible.

  Enter YORK.

YORK.
  How now, sons? What is today's wanton strife?

RICHARD.
  No quarrel, but a slight contention.

YORK.
  About what?

RICHARD.
  About that which concerns your grace and us;
  The crown of England, Mother, which is yours.

YORK.
  Mine, boy? Not till King Henry be dead.
  I took an oath that he should quietly reign.

EDWARD.
  But for a kingdom any oath may be broken.
  I would break a thousand oaths to reign one year.

RICHARD.
  Why do we wait thus? To arms, and now, I say.
  Until the white rose that I wear be dyed
  Even in the lukewarm blood of Henry's heart.

YORK.
  Richard enough.

Enter TUTOR.

What news?

TUTOR.
> The Queen with all the northern earls and lords
> Intend here to besiege you in your castle.
> She is hard by with twenty thousand men.

YORK.
> Think you, that we fear them?
> They are come to Sandal in a happy hour.
> The army of the Queen mean to besiege us?

RICHARD.
> She shall not need. We'll meet her in the field.

YORK.
> What, with five thousand men?

RICHARD.
> Ay, with five hundred, Mother, doe a need.
> A French general? What shall we fear?

EDWARD.
> I hear their drums. Let's see our men in order
> And issue forth and bid them battle straight.

YORK.
> Many a battle did I win in France
> When as the enemy has been ten to one.
> Why should I now not have the same success?
> (*To* RUTLAND.) Tender boy, I must protect you from these quarrels,
> Stay here with our priest.

Exit all but RUTLAND *and* TUTOR.

Enter CLIFFORD.

CLIFFORD.
> Chaplain, away! Your priesthood saves your life.
> As for the brat of this accursed duke,
> Whose mother slew my father, he shall die.

TUTOR.
And I, my lord, will bear him company.

CLIFFORD.
Away with you!

TUTOR.
Ah, Clifford, murder not this innocent child,
Lest you be hated both by God and man.

RUTLAND.
Sweet Clifford, hear me speak before I die.
I am too mean a subject for your wrath.
Be you revenged on men, and let me live.

CLIFFORD.
In vain you speak, poor boy.
Were your brethren here, their lives and yours
Were not revenge sufficient for me.
No, if I dug up your forefathers' graves
And hung their rotten coffins up in chains,
It could not slake mine ire, nor ease my heart.
The sight of any of the house of York.
Is as a fury to torment my soul.
And till I root out your accursed line
And leave not one alive, I live in hell.
Therefore –
(*Lifting his hand.*)
Your mother slew my father, therefore, die.

CLIFFORD *stabs* RUTLAND. *He dies*.

House of York, I come!
And this your son's blood cleaving to my blade
Shall rust upon my weapon, till your blood,
Congealed with this, do make me wipe off both.

Exit all.

Another part of the field near Sandal Castle:

YORK.
The army of the Queen has got the field.
And all my men to the eager foe turn back
And fly, like lambs pursued by hungry wolves.

My sons, God knows what has bechanced them,
But this I know, they have quit themselves
Like men born to renown by life or death.
Three times did Richard make a lane to me.
And thrice cried: 'Courage, Mother! Fight it out!'
And full as oft came Edward to my side,
With purple falchion, painted to the hilt
In blood of those that had encountered him.
And when the hardiest warriors did retire,
Richard cried: 'Charge! And give no foot of ground!'
And cried: 'A crown, or else a glorious tomb!
With this, we charged again, but, out, alas!'
We bodged again.
And now the fatal followers do pursue,
And I am faint and cannot fly their fury.
The sands are numbered that make up my life.
Here must I stay, and here my life must end.

Enter MARGARET, CLIFFORD, PRINCE EDWARD *and* JOAN.

Come, bloody Clifford, I dare your quenchless fury to more rage.

MARGARET.
Yield to our mercy, proud deluded woman.

YORK.
The phoenix, from these my ashes, may bring forth
A bird that will revenge upon you all.
And in that hope I throw mine eyes to heaven,
Scorning whatever you can afflict me with.

CLIFFORD *draws*.

MARGARET.
Hold, valiant Clifford! For a thousand causes
I would prolong awhile the traitor's life.
Speak now, my Prince.

PRINCE EDWARD.
Clifford, do not praise her with such vengeance.
Make it a just and honourable death.

CLIFFORD.
What would Your Grace have done unto her now?

JOAN (*to* MARGARET).
I prayed in France that she should meet a savage death.
She knows not yet the fate of her youngest son.
Please, my prayer is more than answered.

MARGARET.
Come, make her stand upon this molehill here.
Damsel of York, I have you fast!
What? Was it you that would be England's King?
Was it you that reveled in our Parliament?
And made a sermon of your high descent?
Where is your mess of sons to back you now?
The wanton Edward, and Dicky your boy?
Or, where is your darling Rutland?
Look, York: I stained this napkin with the blood
That valiant Clifford, with his rapier's point,
Made issue from the bosom of the boy.
And if your eyes can water for his death,
I give you this to dry your cheeks withal.
Alas poor York, but that I hate you deadly,
I should lament your miserable state.
I pray you, grieve, to make me merry, York.
What, has your fiery heart so parched your entrails
That not a tear can fall for Rutland's death?
York cannot speak, unless she wear a crown.
A crown for York! And, lords, bow low to her.
Hold you her hands, whilst I do set it on.
(*Putting a paper crown on* YORK*'s head.*)
Ay, marry, sir, now looks she like a king!
Ay, this is she that took King Henry's chair,
And this is she was his adopted heir.
But how is it that great House of York.
Is crowned so soon, and broke her solemn oath?
As I bethink me, you should not be king
Till our King Henry had shook hands with death.
O, it's a fault too, too unpardonable!
Off with the crown, and with the crown her head,
And, whilst we breathe, take time to do her dead.

CLIFFORD.
    That is my office, for my father's sake.

MARGARET.
    Nay, stay.
    Let's hear the demonic prayer she makes.

YORK.
    She-wolf of France, but worse than wolves of France,
    Whose tongue's more poison than the adder's tooth!
    How ill-beseeming is it in thy sex
    To triumph, like an Amazonian whore,
    Upon their woes whom fortune captivates.
    It's beauty that does often make women proud,
    But, God he knows, your share thereof is small.
    You are as opposite to every good
    As the Antipodes are to England.
    Women are soft, mild, piteous and flexible,
    You stern, obdurate, flinty, remorseless.
    O tiger's heart wrapped in a woman's hide!
    How could you drain the life-blood of the child?
    To bid the mother wipe her eyes withal,
    And yet be seen to bear a woman's face?
    These tears are my sweet Rutland's obsequies,
    And every drop cries vengeance for his death,
    'Gainst you, foul Clifford, and you, false
    Frenchwoman.

PRINCE EDWARD.
    Beshrew me, but her passion moves me so
    That hardly can I check my eyes from tears.

YORK.
    See, ruthless Queen, a hapless mother's tears.
    This cloth you dipped in blood of my sweet boy,
    And I with tears do wash the blood away.
    Keep you the napkin, and go boast of this.
    And if you tell the heavy story right,
    Upon my soul, the hearers will shed tears.
    Yea even my foes will shed fast-falling tears,
    And say: 'Alas, it was a piteous deed!'
    There, take the crown, and, with the crown, my curse,
    And in your need such comfort come to you

As now I reap at your too cruel hand!
Hard-hearted Clifford, take me from the world.
My soul to heaven, my blood upon your heads!

MARGARET.
Here's to right our gentle-hearted King.

MARGARET *cuts* YORK*'s throat. She dies*.

Off with her head, and set it on York gates,
So York may overlook the town of York.

JOAN (*to* MARGARET).
Brave Queen, the usurpers by you are undone. The Prince is
restored. Lay down your weapons. You have done too much.

MARGARET.
There is a brood of brothers out there still.

Scene Nineteen – Margaret Parleys with the Sons of York

Before city of York.

MARGARET.
Welcome, my lord, to this brave town of York.
Yonder is the head of your arch-enemy
Who sought to be encompassed with your crown.
Does not the object cheer your heart, my lord?

HENRY.
Ay, as the rocks cheer sailors that fear their wreck.
To see this sight, it irks my very soul.

MARGARET.
My gentle husband, this too-much lenity
And harmful pity must be laid aside.
The smallest worm will turn being trodden on.
Look on the boy.
Let his manly face, which promises
Successful fortune, steel your melting heart,
Hold your own, and leave your fears behind.

HENRY.
But, Margaret, tell me, did you never hear
That things ill-got have always bad success?

MARGARET.
My lord, cheer up. Your foes are nigh,
And this soft courage makes your followers faint.
You promised knighthood to our forward son.
Dub him presently.

HENRY.
Edward of Lancaster, arise a knight,
And learn this lesson: draw your sword in right.

PRINCE EDWARD.
My gracious father, by your kingly leave,
I'll draw it as apparent to the crown,
And in that quarrel use it to the death.

MARGARET.
Why, that is spoken like a true prince.

Enter CLIFFORD.

CLIFFORD.
Royal commanders, be in readiness.
For with a band of thirty thousand men
Comes Warwick, backing Edward of York,
And the towns, as they do march along,
Proclaim him King, and many fly to him.
Prepare us our battle, for they are at hand.
(*To* HENRY.) I would Your Highness would depart the
field.
The Queen has best success when you are absent.

MARGARET.
Ay, good my lord, and leave us to our fortune.

Enter EDWARD, RICHARD *and* WARWICK.

EDWARD.
Now, perjured Henry. Wilt you kneel for grace,
And set your diadem upon my head?
Or bide the mortal fortune of the field?

MARGARET.

Go, rate your minions, proud insulting boy!
Becomes it you to be so bold in terms
Before your sovereign and your lawful King?

EDWARD.

I am his King, and he should bow his knee.
I was adopted heir by his consent.
Since when, his oath is broke. For, as I hear,
You, that are King, though he do wear the crown.
You have caused him, by new Act of Parliament,
To blot me out, and put your own son in.

CLIFFORD.

With reason too.
Who should succeed the father but the son?

RICHARD.

Are you there, butcher? It was you that killed
Young Rutland, was it not?

CLIFFORD.

Ay, malignant boy, here I stand to answer you.

MARGARET.

Ay, and I old York – (*Points aloft.*) and yet not satisfied.

RICHARD.

For God's sake, lords, give signal to the fight.

EDWARD.

Peace, brother.

WARWICK.

What says you, Henry, will you yield the crown?

MARGARET.

Why, how now, long-tongued Warwick! Dare you speak?

WARWICK.

Dare you show your face after such viciousness?

HENRY.

Have done with words, my lords, and hear me speak.

MARGARET.

Defy them then, or else hold close your lips.

HENRY.
>I pray, Meg, give no limits to my tongue,
>I am a king, and privileged to speak.

MARGARET.
>My Liege, the wound that bred this meeting here
>Cannot be cured by words, therefore be still.

RICHARD (*aside*).
>Break off this parley, brother, for scarce
>Can I stop from slicing at these child-killers.

EDWARD.
>Say, Henry, shall I have my right, or no?
>A thousand men have broke their fasts today,
>That never shall dine unless you yield the crown.

WARWICK.
>If you say no, their blood upon your head,
>For Edward of York in justice puts his armour on.

PRINCE EDWARD.
>If that be right which Warwick says is right,
>There is no wrong, but everything is right.

RICHARD.
>Whoever fathered you, there your mother stands,
>For, well I wot, you have your mother's tongue.

MARGARET.
>But you are neither like your sire nor dam,
>But like a foul abhorrent stigmatic.

RICHARD.
>Iron of Anjou hid with English gilt,
>Had you been meek, our title still had slept.
>And we, in pity of the gentle King,
>Had slipped our claim until another age.
>Yet, know this, since we have begun to strike,
>We'll never leave till we have hewn you down.

WARWICK.
>This day is born of your relentlessness.

EDWARD.
>Since you deny the gentle King to speak.
>Sound trumpets! Let our bloody banners wave!
>To arms, for either victory, or a grave.

MARGARET.
>Stay, Edward.

EDWARD.
>No, wrangling woman, we'll no longer stay.
>These words will cost ten thousand lives this day.

Scene Twenty – The Battle of Towton

The plains near Towton, the North of England.

MARGARET.
>This vantage point at Castle Hill Wood grants
>A clear view across the windy Towton plain,
>Hear you the forces as they assemble?
>Each hears the rattle of their armour,
>But neither has set eyes upon the other.
>When Edward's troops advance below,
>We ambush.
>Set our men to quiet preparations.

CLIFFORD.
>They're weak and tired from their march.
>They cannot outpace our pursuit.
>This sleeted day frowns, and Edward's sun is clouded.

Another part of the field:

Enter EDWARD, RICHARD and WARWICK.

RICHARD.
>Say, Warwick, how fares your number?
>Noble gentlemen are giving up the ghost,
>There, underneath the belly of their steeds
>That stain their fetlocks in this smoking blood.
>Cry out: 'Revenge, brother, revenge, Mother!'

WARWICK.

I'm troubled. The day is in the balance.
Here on my knee I vow to God above
I'll never pause, never stand still
Till either death has closed these eyes of mine
Or fortune given me justice for England.

EDWARD.

O, Warwick, I do bend my knee with yours,
And in this vow do chain my soul to you.

Another part of the field:

Enter HUME, *with a slain soldier.*

HUME.

This man, whom hand to hand I slew, who knew?
May be possessed with some small store of crowns,
And I, happily take them from him now,
To profit from the ill wind that slices
Through this limb-strewn, bloodstained hell-loosed
kingdom.
Who's this? O God, it is my father's face,
Whom in this conflict I unawares have killed.
Pardon me, God, I knew not what I did,
And pardon, Father, for I knew you not.
My tears shall wipe away these bloody marks,
I've no more words till they have flowed their fill.

HENRY.

O piteous spectacle! O bloody times!
The red rose and the white are on her face,
The fatal colours of our striving houses.
The one her purple blood right well resembles,
The other her pale cheeks, methinks, presents.
Wither one rose, and let the other flourish.
If we contend, a thousand lives must wither.
Sad-hearted woman, much overgone with care,
Here sits a king more woeful than even you are.

Another part of the field:

Enter CLIFFORD, *injured.*

CLIFFORD.
Here burns my candle out, ay, here it dies.
Which, while it lasted gave King Henry light.
O, Lancaster, I fear your overthrow
More than my body parting with my soul.
The air hath got into my deadly wounds
And much effuse of blood does make me faint.
Come, Edward and Richard, Warwick and the rest,
I stabbed your brother's bosom – split my breast.

Enter EDWARD, RICHARD *and* WARWICK.

EDWARD.
Whose soul is this who takes his heavy leave?
See who it is and now the battle's ended
If friend or foe, let him be gently used.

RICHARD.
Revoke that rule of mercy, for it's Clifford!

WARWICK.
Speak, Clifford, do you know who speaks to you?

RICHARD.
Clifford, ask mercy and obtain no grace.

EDWARD.
Clifford, devise excuses for your faults.

RICHARD.
Where's Captain Margaret to fence you now?
Ay, he's but dead.

WARWICK.
Margaret has fled and Henry is captured.
Bring him to the Tower closely guarded.
And now, Edward, to London with triumphant march,
And there to be crowned England's Royal King!

Scene Twenty-One – The Aftermath on Towton Field

The snowy winter hill at Towton. Palm Sunday.

Enter MARGARET *with* JOAN. *Church bells peal in the distance.*

MARGARET.
My enemy flies south in hot pursuit of me.
They have the King. Yet I remain, to respect the field.

JOAN (*to* MARGARET).
Blessings on each soul this holy day.

MARGARET.
I want just notice of the numbers dead. For both our houses.
This blanket of snow blinds us to the bloody truth. Fellow!
Come here to me! Yo! Come here at once.

Enter HUME.

It is against the noble laws of war to strip the bodies of the dead. How does your conscience let you do this on this holy day?

HUME.
The sleet has turned to snow, the light will soon be gone.
I must eat. Ill blows the wind that profits nobody.

MARGARET.
There is not a boy left alive under the snow. The muster-files list men from twelve to seventy. And here they lie, hacked down, dismembered, dead. This slaughter is no marketplace for greed. Where is your God?

HUME.
I must work how I can in this country.

MARGARET.
Cold is my anger since I employed you last. Work for me,
Hume, in the task at hand. I will reward you.

HUME.
How do you know me? The war years have marked my jaw, ravaged my skin.
Long gone are the days since I ran with Jack Cade.

MARGARET.
Work for me now. Wander over this Towton field. Look at
our dead. List this carnage of nobles and common men.
Entire English families lie drowned in their own blood.
Hapless bands of brothers run through with English steel.
Kill the wounded horses. Silence the field. Bury the bodies.

HUME.
The ground is frozen, Majesty.

MARGARET.
You will find a way.

JOAN (*to* MARGARET).
Why did you fight on Palm Sunday?

MARGARET.
You attacked Paris on Ascension Day, though you were
damned for it.

JOAN (*to* MARGARET).
That is why I lost. I was defeated without God. Your father
carried me from the field.

MARGARET.
We put our quarrel to the will of heaven, now a carpet of men
lie here, cut down, frozen like rock to this fortress nation.

HUME.
Will you sing a hymn with me?

Under the level winter sky
I saw a thousand Christs go by.
They sang an idle song and free
As they went up to calvary.

Careless of eye and coarse of lip,
They marched in holiest fellowship.
That heaven might heal the world, they gave
Their earth-born dreams to deck the grave.

I saw ten thousand Christs go by
The marching men of Towton.

With souls unpurged and steadfast breath
They supped the sacrament of death.

And for each one, far off, apart,
Seven swords have rent a woman's heart.

MARGARET *breaks*.

I saw twenty thousand Christs go by
The marching men of Towton.

I saw thirty thousand Christs go by
The marching men of Towton.

JOAN (*to* MARGARET).
No battle in France ever cost this many lives. So many
Lancastrian nobles died today. Where is chivalry? Virtue?
Justice? This kind of warfare is a savage thing. You have
become English.

MARGARET.
My sore heart weeps for my adopted country, this land of
such dear souls, but I must away, fetch Edward and find safe
haven in Scotland. This bloody wound may make some
sense to us tomorrow. We will regroup.

Scene Twenty-Two – Margaret Makes an Alliance

The Scottish borders. Berwick Castle.

MARGARET.
Warwick, you are a traitor to the King.

WARWICK.
I come in kindness and unfeigned love.
(*Offers cheese and wine*.)
Let me unfold my tale and you can judge.

MARGARET.
Get to it. What deal have you?

WARWICK.
I have here a stolen letter from Richard /

HUME (*aside*).
 Nothing to do with me.

WARWICK.
 / to Edward, the usurping King
 (*Reads*.) 'The Earl of Warwick and King Lewis of France,
 Are so weak in courage and in judgement
 That they will take no offence at our abuse.'

MARGARET.
 Ha! What abuse? Have they played you for sport?
 Come, Edward, stand with me this next cold hour.
 Join me in this conversation with our foe.
 Where is your mocking monarch and does he know you are
 here?

WARWICK.
 England's lawful King languishes in the Tower.

MARGARET.
 Ha! Has some band of brigands captured him on my behalf?

WARWICK.
 You miss my drift. Henry is my royal King.

MARGARET.
 I need not bear witness to mockery.
 Impudent and shameless Warwick! What jest is this?

PRINCE EDWARD (*aside*).
 Dissemble, Mother, keep your dauntless mind
 Sharp against all of her dishonesties. This is a ploy.

WARWICK.
 He is no more my King, for he dishonours me,
 I here renounce Edward and return to Henry.
 My noble Queen, let former grudges pass,
 And henceforth I am your true servitor.
 I will revenge his wrong to Henry,
 And replant the King in his former state.

JOAN (*to* MARGARET).
 How can Warwick be welcome in your presence?
 This woman who despaired that I might live,
 Stood on the platform, adding pitch and tar.

MARGARET (*aside*).
    Warwick has never been a dark soul,
    She placed barrels of pitch upon the fatal stake
    So that your torture could be shortened.
    She still follows the chilvalric code.
    And has long built alliances where she must.
    (*To* WARWICK.) Speak on.

WARWICK.
    The unlawful King, Edward of York,
    Is the body of this text:
    (*Reads*.) 'King Lewis of France will become your enemy for
    mocking him.'

MARGARET.
    What mock?

WARWICK.
    There was a long-held deal that Lady Bona of France
    Would marry Edward once broils were done,
    Thus England would not drift back into war.
    Edward of York has married another:
    A match with her that brings no advantage.

MARGARET.
    Proud setter-up and puller-down of kings!
    This was your deal they have callously undone.

WARWICK.
    This has shamed me across France,
    All courts of Europe talk of nothing else.
    And dark days ahead for England are foretold.

MARGARET.
    Ha! What can I do?
    There is no Lancastrian force left.
    Towton stole thirty thousand souls from England.

WARWICK.
    You represent the people of England.
    (*Reads*.) 'God forbid that Warwick join with France in such
    alliance.
    She would have more strength than the commonwealth.'
    We two are an alliance they would never dream.

With my soldiers from Calais, and King Lewis's men,
You gathering what you can from villages and counties,
Together we will be a force that can settle this.
The only future for England is with Henry.
God is my witness, my oath is true.

JOAN (*to* MARGARET).
I was sent with few men
And little hope of success, to a battle I could not win,
To destroy me in the eyes of the people.

MARGARET *paces*.

MARGARET.
Warwick, these words may turn my hate to love,
And I may forgive and forget old faults,
If joy that you become King Henry's friend
Can conjure itself truly in my heart.

HUME (*aside*).
I wouldn't bet on it.

WARWICK.
Majesty, I humbly beg your forgiveness.

PRINCE EDWARD.
Mother, caution is our vanguard, be warned.

MARGARET.
Dear, dear men of Towton, my mourning weeds are laid aside,
And I am ready to put armour on.

HUME.
What?

MARGARET.
To London, the Tower with your garrison from Calais,
We will follow to the west with the French King's army,
Yet, before you go, answer me one final doubt,
What pledge have we of your firm loyalty?

WARWICK.
This shall assure my constant loyalty,
That if Your Majesty and this young prince agree,

I'll join mine eldest daughter and my joy
To him forthwith in holy wedlock bands.

PRINCE EDWARD.
Mother, why?

MARGARET.
Yes, I agree, and thank you for your motion.
She is fair and virtuous, therefore delay not,
I give my blessing to Warwick this hour,
And, with my hand, my faith irrevocable.
My only son and Warwick's daughter shall be one.

PRINCE EDWARD.
If Your Majesty decrees, I accept.

They shake. WARWICK *exits.*

MARGARET.
Warwick was the chief that raised Edward to the crown,
But I'll be chief to bring him crashing down.

JOAN.
This is an ill-starred assembly.

HUME.
For fuck's sake.

Scene Twenty-Three – Margaret Marches on Tewkesbury

Country roads in the South West of England.

MARGARET.
Where is Edward of York? Send scouts! How can a noble
war be fought in the dark?

HUME.
I know his movements. But I fear to speak.

MARGARET.
Speak, Hume, England is waiting.

HUME.

> They know you have ten thousand strong. They know your
> intent is set for Tewkesbury. To cross the bridge at Worcester
> you must march all night. Gather yourself. Gather your son.

PRINCE EDWARD.

> Methinks the power that Edward has in the field will never
> be enough to counter us. Do not doubt us, Hume. My father
> is King. We are here to restore him.

MARGARET.

> Edward's strength is true, sweet prince. Stealth and cunning
> as well as your prayers must we call to our aid now. Bring
> the scouts to me, smoke out the spies, now we march.
> (*To* HUME.) Send posts. Inform them that we march to
> London. Confuse their expectations. We will to Tewkesbury
> tonight.

Another part of the field:

EDWARD *and* RICHARD.

EDWARD.

> Richard, those powers that the Queen
> Has raised have arrived on our coast.
> And, as we hear, march on to fight with us.

RICHARD.

> The Queen is valued ten thousand strong,
> And the Welsh nobles will soon flock to her.
> If she have time to breathe be well assured
> Her faction will be full as strong as ours.

EDWARD.

> The trap is set. Warwick must fall this coming day.
> March how you can, without Warwick they die.
> I pray this day for one single outcome, that
> this hand, fast wound about her coal-black hair
> Will, while her head is warm and new cut off,
> Write in the dust this sentence with her blood,
> 'Wind-changing Warwick, now can change no more.'
> Come, we are informed by our scouts and spies.
> That they do hold their course toward Tewksbury.
> And, as we march, our strength will be augmented

In every county as we go along.
Strike up the drum! Cry 'Courage!' and away.

Another part of the field:

MARGARET.
What news of Warwick? Does she have the King?

HUME.
Madam, the news is fearful and ill-omened. On her way to
London to set the crown upon King Henry's head, she was
betrayed, met with an ambush, her body yielded to the earth.

JOAN *conjures* WARWICK*'s death for* MARGARET.

JOAN.
Lady of Anjou, she was the last of my foes, yet I find no
peace. Her eyes that were as piercing as the midday sun are
now cold-dimmed with death's black veil. Despite the cold
congealed blood that glued her lips and would not let her
speak, she whispered as her soul left her body: 'Farewell to
all, we'll meet again in heaven.' I will see her there, God
willing, when this purgatory ends.

MARGARET.
This is a soul dark mournful day. She was for England, and
I was late to see her worth. She sought the secret treasons of
the world, and followed fearlessly to the righteous cause.
This battle is now no longer yours. Leave me to my fate
alone, French spirit. Rest in peace, release yourself from my
world, until we meet again.

JOAN.
Mine was a quest, but this debased slaughter cannot be sated.
There is no end. I go.

MARGARET.
I am the black and threatening cloud newly blown on shore
to shroud the sun of York. With London lost, we must make
Tewkesbury tonight. This race is not yet run.

PRINCE EDWARD.
Be else a hero or death comes quick. I have my sword,
Mother!

Another part of the field:

RICHARD.
> The loyal mayor of Worcester has refused the Queen
> To cross the bridge. They have a further ten miles to march.

EDWARD.
> We will be in Tewkesbury before her.
> This day thrills the House of York, my brother!

Another part of the field:

MARGARET.
> Here pitch our battle, hence we will not budge.
> Lords, knights, and gentlemen, what I should say
> My tears gainsay, for every word I speak,
> You see, I drink the water of my eyes.
> Therefore, no more but this: Henry, your sovereign,
> Is prisoner to the foe, his state usurped,
> His realm a slaughterhouse, his subjects slain,
> His statutes cancelled and his treasure spent.
> And yonder is the wolf that makes this spoil.
> You fight in justice, then, in God's name, lords,
> Be valiant and give signal to the fight!

Scene Twenty-Four – Margaret is Captured

Plains near Tewkesbury.

EDWARD.
> Now here ends this period of tumultuous broils.
> For the commoners, send them back to their counties.

HUME.
> For my part, I'll not leave my royal mistress.
> I meet my fortune with hers.

EDWARD.
> A rough kind of warrior, still with some fight?

MARGARET.
   Get you hence to Ipswich. This is not for you.

HUME.
   No, madam, my home is with you.

EDWARD.
   Proclamation is made, that who finds Edward
   Shall have a high reward.

Enter RICHARD *with* PRINCE EDWARD.

RICHARD.
   It is, and lo, where youthful Edward comes!

EDWARD (*to* RICHARD).
   Richard ho! The fighting is at an end.

PRINCE EDWARD.
   Mother! You live!

MARGARET.
   Stand tall, my boy. God is on your side.

EDWARD.
   Bring forth the gallant, let us hear him speak.
   Edward of Lancaster, what satisfaction can you make,
   For bearing arms, for stirring up my subjects,
   And all the trouble you have turned me to?

PRINCE EDWARD.
   Speak like a subject, proud Edward of York!
   Believe that I am now my father's mouth.
   Resign your chair, and where I stand you kneel,
   Whilst I propose the selfsame words to you.

MARGARET.
   Ah, that your father had been so resolved!

RICHARD.
   That you might still have worn the petticoat,
   And never stole the britches from King Henry!

PRINCE EDWARD.
   Finally, you address my father properly.

RICHARD.
I will finally address your sweet dad.
By heaven, brat, I'll plague you for those words.

MARGARET.
Ay, you were born to be a plague to men.
Hence, heap of wrath, foul indigested lump.
(*To* EDWARD.) Better to have aborted this whelp than have
let him live.

RICHARD.
For God's sake, take away this captive scold.

PRINCE EDWARD.
Nay, take away this odious malcontent.

EDWARD.
Peace, wilful boy, or I will charm your tongue.

RICHARD.
Untutored lad, you are too malapert.

PRINCE EDWARD.
I know my duty. You are all undutiful.
Lascivious Edward, and you, malicious Dick,
I tell you all, I am your better, traitors that you are,
And you usurped my father's right and mine.

RICHARD.
Take that, you likeness of this railer here.

Stabs him.

Writhing? Take that, to end your agony.

Stabs him again.

MARGARET.
No, no, no, no. no.
O, kill me too! Before the truth of this
Strikes at the root of my heart.

RICHARD.
Marry an' shall.

Offers to kill her.

EDWARD.
Hold, Richard, hold, for we have done too much.

RICHARD.
Why should she live, to fill the world with words?

MARGARET.
Breathe, my boy, breathe.
O Ned, sweet Ned. Speak to your mother, boy.
Can you not speak? What's this that bubbles on your breath?
O God see not this, do not suffer it!
My sweet son, ruler of your father's future.
A crown that was won with blood, lost be it so.
No, no my heart will burst, and if I speak,
And I will speak, that so my heart may burst.
O but remember this accursed day,
When you have split my very heart with sorrow.
Witness my son, now in the shade of death,
Whose bright outshining beams your cloudy wrath
Has in eternal darkness folded up.
True men never spend their fury on a child.
What's worse than 'murderer' that I may name it?
O traitors! Murderers! Butchers and villains!

RICHARD.
Margaret, excuse me to the King, my brother.
I'll hence to London on a serious matter.
Before long, you'll be sure to hear some news.

MARGARET.
Stay, devil. I know your tricks.

RICHARD.
The Tower, the Tower.

Exit RICHARD.

MARGARET.
Anger is my meat. I gorge upon it.
I shall feed upon this crime against heaven.
Shamefully my hopes by you are butchered.
My charity is outrage, life my shame,
And in that shame will live my sorrow's rage!

Proud Edward, do: usurper, dare you do it?
That I may join my son in God's holy sight.

EDWARD.

Away with her, and waft her hence to France.

MARGARET.

So come to you and yours, as to this Prince!

EDWARD.

Where's Richard gone?

MARGARET.

To London, all in haste. It is my guess
To make a bloody supper in the Tower.

EDWARD.

He's sudden, if a thing comes in his head.

Scene Twenty-Five – Richard Visits the King in the Tower

London. The Tower.

RICHARD.

Good day, my lord. What, at your book so hard?

HENRY.

What scene of death has Richard now to act?
Wherefore do you come? Is it for my life?
Kill me with your weapon, not with words!
My breast can better brook your dagger's point
Than can my aged ears, your heinous boasts.

RICHARD.

Thinks you I am an executioner?

HENRY.

A persecutor I am sure you are.

RICHARD.

Your son I killed, for his presumption.

HENRY.

The owl shrieked at your birth – an evil sign,
The night-crow cried, aboding luckless time,
Dogs howled, and hideous tempest shook down trees,
The raven rooked her on the chimney's top,
And chattering magpies in dismal discords sung.
Your mother felt more than a mother's pain,
And yet brought forth less than a mother's hope.
To wit, an indigested rotted lump,
Not like the fruit of such a goodly tree.
And if the rest be true which I have heard,
You came –

RICHARD.

I'll hear no more. Die, prophet, in your speech.
(*Stabs him.*)
For this act, amongst the rest, was I ordained.

HENRY.

Ay, and for much more slaughter after this.
O, God forgive my sins and pardon you!

HENRY *dies*.

RICHARD.

What? Will the aspiring blood of Lancaster
Sink in the ground? I thought it would have mounted.

I, have neither pity, love, nor fear.
Indeed, it's true what Henry told me of.
For I have often heard my mother say
I came into the world with my legs forward.
The midwife wondered: and the women cried:
'O, Jesus bless us, he is born with teeth!'
And so I was, which plainly signified
That I should snarl, and bite, and play the dog,
Then, since the heavens have shaped my body so,
Let hell make crooked my mind to answer it.
And this word 'love', which greybeards call divine,
Be resident in men like one another,
And not in me! I am myself alone.

Scene Twenty-Six – The Queen of England Sails into Exile

Dover. A dockside, a gangplank.

HUME.
I must stay here and make my honest way.
England is mine.

MARGARET.
Mine too.
Heaven bless you and keep you, Hume. Farewell.

MARGARET *boards the ship. Ships' bells ring, foghorn sounds.*

This barge with drowsy, slow and flagging sails,
That drags me through this melancholy night,
Breathes foul contagious darkness in my soul.
I do find more pain in banishment
Than death can yield me here.

Poor Margaret will away from England, her home.
I have grown away from chivalry, virtue, France, and God.
Why should I now return to Anjou?
I have lost Henry, Edward and all my world.
I will die neither mother, wife, nor England's Queen.
I have lived longer in England than ever I lived in France,
I have eaten more English mutton than ever I ate French veal.
Edward of York, I wish your rule success.
But maybe I am a prophet, Richard will cut you down.
This sorrow that I have, by right is his,
And all the pleasures he usurps are mine.
If heaven have any grievous plague in store
Exceeding those that I can wish (not pray) upon him,
O let them keep it till his sins be ripe,
And then hurl down their indignation
On him, the troubler of the poor world's peace!
Richard, you are the loathèd issue of your mother's loins!
A bottled spider.
Foul shame upon you!
Cancel his bond of life, dear God, I plead,
That I may live and say: 'The dog is dead.'

This land of such dear souls, this dear, dear land,
Torn through with ancient bitterness and wanton rage,
What have we done?
This England that was wont to conquer others,
Has made a shameful conquest of itself.

The End.